ANTICHRIST

Cardinal Roberti Bellarmini S.R.E. Presbyteri Cardinalis Archiepiscopi Capuani

Leodij I. Valdor sculpsit

De Controversiis

ON ANTICHRIST

by
St. Robert Bellarmine, S.J.
Doctor of the Church

Translated from the Latin
by
Ryan Grant
with a foreword by
Fr. Philip Wolfe, F.S.S.P.

MEDIATRIX PRESS

www.mediatrixpress.com

ISBN-10: 0692648917
ISBN-13: 978-0692648919

Translated from *De Controversiis Fidei Christianae, vol. 1, De Romano Pontifice, liber III*, 1590 Sartorius Publishers, Ingolstadt. Revised according to the edition published in Prague, 1721.

Mediatrix Press
607 E. 6th Ave.
Post Falls, ID 83854

Cover art: *The Deeds of Antichrist,* detail.
-Lorenzo Signarelli
Orvieto Cathedral, Italy, 1517.

TABLE OF CONTENTS

FOREWORD ix

CHAPTER I
A Disputation is Proposed on Antichrist 1

CHAPTER II
Antichrist is Going to be a Certain, Specific Man
. . . . 7

CHAPTER III
It is Shown That Antichrist has not yet Come. . . . 19

CHAPTER IV
*The First proof: the Rule of Antichrist has not yet
Begun.* 31

CHAPTER V
*The Second Proof: Desolation of the Roman
Empire* 37

CHAPTER VI
A Third Proof: Enoch and Elijah 45

CHAPTER VII
The Fourth Proof: the Persecution of Antichrist
. . . . 53

CHAPTER VIII
The Fifth Proof: the Duration of Antichrist 57

CHAPTER IX
The Sixth Proof: the End of the World 65

CHAPTER X
On the Name "Antichrist" 69

CHAPTER XI
On the Mark of Antichrist. 79

CHAPTER XII
On the Begetting of Antichrist. 85

CHAPTER XIII
On the Seat of Antichrist. 93

CHAPTER XIV
On the Doctrine of Antichrist 107

CHAPTER XV
On the Miracles of Antichrist 119

CHAPTER XVI
On the Kingdom and Battles of Antichrist . . . 125

CHAPTER XVII
On Gog and Magog 131

CHAPTER XVIII
*The Absurdities of the Heretics are Refuted, in
Which They not only try to Show, but Impudently
Declare that the Roman Pontiff is Antichrist* . 143

CHAPTER XIX

    The Trifles of the Smalchaldich Council of the
    Lutherans are Refuted 147

CHAPTER XX

    The Lies of Calvin are Refuted 153

CHAPTER XXI

    The Lies of Illyricus are Refuted 157

CHAPTER XXII

    The Ineptitude of Tilman is Refuted 175

CHAPTER XXIII

    The Lies of Chytraeus are Refuted 179

CHAPTER XXIV

    The Arguments of Calvin and Illyricus are
    Refuted, Where the Former Tries to Show the
    Pope is no Longer a Bishop, and the Latter on the
    Fable of "Pope Joan" 209

FOREWORD

✠

JMJ

HIS book on the Antichrist, penned by a great Doctor of the Church, is a real jewel. For years I have preached from the original Latin version of this work, because in one small volume, St Robert Bellarmine has assembled an incredible amount of solid—and oftentimes amazing—information, drawn from Sacred Tradition and the authentic understanding of Scripture, on this mysterious and most disturbing man and his times.

It is certainly an opportune moment for the publication of this translation. Over the course of my priesthood, it has become more and more apparent that many Catholics here in the US have already succumbed to Protestant errors in eschatology, under the influence of best-sellers like the Hal Lindsey books, the Left Behind books and movies, or television preachers—and with the 500th anniversary of Fr Luther's revolt looming, and given the strange goings-on at the Holy See, the times are ripe for another round of the traditional Protestant attacks on the Papacy. Although St Robert had already refuted a great many of their errors, until today, this work remained inaccessible to the average Catholic.

Personally, I am also delighted that the eschatological mission of the Holy Fathers Enoch and Elijah, so well testified to in Sacred Tradition, but virtually forgotten in our day and age, will become more widely known.

We owe a real debt of gratitude to Ryan Grant for bringing this work to a wider audience. I pray that it receives a very wide reading.

Fr Phil Wolfe FSSP
Tyler, Texas
Chair of St Peter in Antioch 2016

ANTICHRIST

CHAPTER I
A Disputation is Proposed on Antichrist

Up to this point we have proved that the Roman Pontiff succeeds Peter in the supreme rule of the whole Church. It remains that we should see whether at some time the Roman Pontiff might have fallen from that degree; certainly our adversaries contend that at this time, there is not a true bishop of Rome, whatever he might have been before. Even Nilos Cabásilas of Thessalonika, at the end of his little book against the primacy of the Roman Pontiff, says: "But the chief and principal point of my discourse is that as long as the Pope shall preserve the heavenly and agreeable order formerly instituted in the Church, as long as he shall adhere to Christ, the supreme Lord and head of the Church, I shall easily suffer him both as head of the Church and high Priest, even the successor of Peter or the Apostles; I will allow that all obey him, and that nothing should diminish that which pertains to his honor; but if he would have fallen from truth, nor wished to return to it, then rightly he ought to be held for one condemned and cast out." Thus Nilos.

But he ought to have shown into what errors the Roman Pontiffs have fallen, as well as both when and by whom they were condemned. Certainly we know that in the General Council of the Lateran under Innocent III, Lyons under Gregory X, and Florence under Eugene IV, the Greeks were convicted of error and returned to the faith of the Latins. Thereafter, they always went back to their

1

vomit, and for that reason were gravely punished by God. Yet we read nowhere that the Latins ever came to the faith of the Greeks. Nor can any ecclesiastical judgment be brought against the Latins, as we have brought many against the Greeks.

On the other hand, Calvin says: "Let us grant all these things are true (although we have already forced the contrary from them): Peter was constituted head of the universal Church by the voice of Christ, and that honor being conferred upon him, he laid down in the Roman See, and it was ratified by the authority of the ancient Church, confirmed by long use, that the Roman Pontiff always had supreme power over all, and was in his person the judge of all cases and men, and was subject to the judgment of none; let them have many more if they want. I respond that still, in one word, it will avail them nothing, except that there ought to be a Church and a bishop in Rome."[1] And below that: "Let the Romans untie this knot: I deny that the pontiff is the prince of bishops, since he is not really a bishop."[2] And further: "Rome was rightly the mother of all churches once, but from the time it began to be the seat of Antichrist, it ceased to be that which it was."[3] And again: "We appear to some to be cursed and petulant since we call the Roman Pontiff Antichrist; but they who think so do not understand that they charge Paul with immodesty, after whom we speak; nay more, we speak thus from his own mouth. And lest anyone would cast before us words of Paul which might pertain to another matter and wrongly distort them away from the Roman Pontiff, I will show briefly that it can be understood

---

[1]   *Instit.*, lib. 4, ch. 7, § 23.

[2]   *Ibid.*, §24.

[3]   *Ibid.*

in no manner other than that the papacy is the seat of Antichrist."[4]

All the heretics of this time teach similar things: Firstly, Luther, in his computation of the times, as well as in his *Assertions*, article 28 and 36, and often in other places. Likewise the Lutheran Centuriators in all of their *Centuries*;[5] Illyricus in his book on the Primacy; David Chytraeus in his work on the Apocalypse (the ninth and thirteenth chapters); Wolfgang Musculus in his work *de Ecclesia*, in common citations; Theodore Beza;[6] Theodore Bibliander;[7] Heinrich Pantaleon in his *Chronologia*; Henry Bullinger in his preface to his homilies on the Apocalypse, and above all, John Wycliff, who is among those condemned in article 30 of the Council of Constance, sess. 8. All of these pronounced that the Pontiff is the Antichrist.

Therefore, in order that this question should be carefully explained, it will be treated in nine chapters. The first will be on the name of Antichrist. The second on whether Antichrist might be one man, or a race of men. Thirdly, on the time of his coming and his death. Fourth, on his proper name. Fifth, from which nation he is going to be born, and especially by whom he will be received. Sixth, where he is going to set up his seat. Seventh, on his doctrine and morals. Eighth, on his miracles. Ninth, on his kingdom and battles. From all these it will appear very clearly with what impudence the heretics make the Roman Pontiff out to be the Antichrist, in which we will add a chapter proving not only that the Roman Pontiff is not

---

[4] *Ibid.,* §25.

[5] *Centur. 1*, lib. 2, ch. 4, column 434, and in all subsequent books of the centuries.

[6] Beza, *Commentario 2 Thessalon.,* 2.

[7] *Chronicum*, tabul. 10, 11, 12, 13 & 14.

Antichrist, but that he could by no means cease to be the bishop and shepherd of the whole Church, and such that no part of the objections of Calvin shall remain unanswered.

Now in regard to the first, some of our adversaries teach that the name "Antichrist" properly means Vicar of Christ, and hence the Pope, who asserts he is the Vicar of Christ, is himself Antichrist. Wolfgang Musculus teaches this in his citations, in the chapter on the power of ministers, and he tries to show that the word ἀντὶ means in place of, so, ἀντὶχριστος is in place of Christ, just as ἀντιορατηγὸς means he who thrusts himself in place of a leader, that is, one who would have it that he is the vicar of a leader. The Centuriators also teach that the Pope is the true Antichrist because he makes himself the Vicar of Christ.

But without a doubt they are deceived or are trying to deceive. The name "Antichrist" can not mean Vicar of Christ in any manner, rather, it merely means someone contrary to Christ; not contrary in any way whatever, but so much so that he will fight against that which pertains to the seat and dignity of Christ; that is, one who will be a rival of Christ and to be held as Christ, after he who truly is Christ has been cast out.

The meaning of this noun is proved in three ways. Firstly, because in Greek, the term ἀντὶ properly means opposition, and they are said to be opposed not only to those among whom they oppose, but even those whom they exert influence over. From there, it comes to pass that ἀντί, in composition, sometimes means contrariety and sometimes equivalence but never subordination, as is clear in the examples of all such names. For instance, ἀντὶπαλος means imitation in mourning; ἀντίδοτον, a contrary remedy; αντιφρασις contradiction; αντιοροφος equivalence;

ἀντίθεος equal to God; ἀντιχειρις, that is the thumb, because from that region it is opposed and rules the rest of the hand, and so on and so forth. But "vicar" does not mean opposition but subordination to another thing, and therefore, cannot be expressed through the term ἀντὶ.

Hence, the term ἀντιστρατηγὸς does not mean the vicar of a leader but ordinarily a contrary leader just as ἀντισρατενομαι is a civil war. Moreover, sometimes one who is in place of a leader is not subject to him but rather equal to him in the way that the Latin words *Propraetor*, or *Proconsul*, do not mean the vicar of a praetor, or a consul, but one who is in some province, like that which a praetor or a consul is in the city. And in this Musculus was deceived because he read with Budaeus that ἀντισρατηγὸς means a propraetor, and he reckoned it meant vicar of a praetor, which is false.

Secondly, the same is proven from Scripture. Although there is some ambiguity about this noun still, as it is received in Scripture it is not ambiguous; our question ought not to be on the term ἀντιχριστος in an absolute sense, but as it is found in the Scriptures. Next, in the Scriptures the one who is called Antichrist is he: "who is extolled above everything which is called God."[8] That is certainly not a Vicar of Christ but an enemy of Christ, the true God. In the First Epistle of John, Antichrist is said to be he "who denies Jesus is the Messiah,"[9] i.e. he who denies Jesus is the Christ, that he would claim for himself that which is for Christ. And in Matthew, it is said that Antichrist will affirm himself to be Christ,[10] which can hardly be a vicar but rather would be an imitator.

---

[8]   2 Thessalonians 2:4.

[9]   1 John 2:22.

[10]   Matt. 24:5, 24.

Thirdly, from all the authors who wrote on Antichrist and from the common consensus of all Christians, we understand by "Antichrist" a certain man as a distinct Pseudochrist. This is how St. John Damascene explains this term from the Greek Fathers,[11] and in the same manner Jerome explains it from the Latin Fathers,[12] and he was also an expert in the Greek language.

Next, Henry Stephan gives a similar explanation in his *Treasury on the Greek Language*, albeit he is from the number of the Swiss heretics. Thus, we have our first argument against our adversaries. Since the noun "Antichrist" means an enemy and imitator of Christ, and the Roman Pontiff is from the household of Christ declaring that he is subject to Christ in all things, it is clear that he would in no way say he is Christ, or that he makes himself equal to him; therefore, it is manifest that he is not Antichrist.

---

[11] *De Fide*, lib. 4, ch. 28.

[12] *Quaestione undecima, ad Algasiam.*

CHAPTER II
Antichrist is Going to be a Certain, Specific Man

NOW in what pertains to the second, we agree with our adversaries in one thing and differ in another. We agree in the fact that just as the name of Christ is received in two ways, sometimes properly concerning the specific and individual person of Christ, who is Jesus of Nazareth, and sometimes commonly concerning all those who have a similitude with Christ in regard to anointing, just as all priests, prophets and kings are said to be of Christ: "Do not touch my Christs;"[1] so also Antichrist is received properly sometimes for a certain distinct enemy of Christ, on which the Scriptures teach, and sometimes commonly for all who oppose Christ in some way. We read in the First Epistle of John: "You have heard, that Antichrist is coming, and now there are many Antichrists;"[2] in other words, you have heard Antichrist is going to come, and now, although that singular Antichrist has not yet come, still many seducers have come who also can be called Antichrists.

But we differ on Antichrist properly so called, whether he might be one individual man. All Catholics think that Antichrist is one specific man; but all the heretics cited

---

[1] Psalm 104 (105):15 We have rendered Christ directly to retain the sense of the original, the term in Greek (Χριστός) means "anointed", and thus Jesus, the anointed one, the culmination of every precursor of "anointing" in the Old Testament. -Translator's note.

[2] 1 John 2:18.

above teach that Antichrist, properly so called, is not a single person but a single throne of a tyrannical kingdom as well as the seat of its apostasy that presides over the Church.

The Centuriators say: "The Apostles teach that Antichrist is not only one person, but a whole kingdom through false teachers in the temple of God that is presiding in the Church, in a great city, i.e. the city of Rome, whose works are compared to the deception and deceit of the devil."[3] The others we cited say similar things.

These are their reasons. First, Paul says that already in his time Antichrist began to live in the world: "The mystery of iniquity is now operating,"[4] and still he says in the same place that Antichrist must be killed by Christ at the end of the world. Hence, Beza concludes in his commentary on this citation in Thessalonians that: "They are clearly hallucinating when they think this can be understood about one man; unless they give me someone who remains alive from the age of Paul even to the day of judgment." Calvin argues in the same way from this passage. They confirm this reasoning from John who, in his First Epistle, says: "Every spirit that denies Jesus, it is not from God and this is Antichrist whom you have heard is coming, and is now in the world."[5]

The second reason is of Beza: because Daniel 7 does not understand individuals by the individual names of the beasts of bear, lion and leopard, but rather individual kingdoms, one of which contains many kings. Therefore, Paul, who wondrously agrees with Daniel, does not understand the man of sin and the son of perdition as one

---

[3] *Cent. 1*, lib. 2, ch. 4, colum. 435.

[4] 2 Thessalonians 2:7.

[5] 1 John 4:3.

individual person but a figure as a body of many tyrants.

The third reason is of Calvin who argues from what is said in 1 John 2 that those who believe that one man is going to be Antichrist are mad and err of their own accord, since Paul in 2 Thessalonians 2 wrote that apostasy was coming and his head is going to be Antichrist. Accordingly, apostasy is a certain general defection from the faith which indeed makes one body and one rule, and is not a matter of a few years that it could be completed under one king.

With all of these not withstanding, the truth is that Antichrist is one individual man. The fact is proven from all the Scriptures and the Fathers who treat on Antichrist. There are five passages of Scripture. The first is in the Gospel of John: "I have come in the name of my Father, and you did not receive me, if another will have come in his own name, you will receive him."[6] Musculus and Calvin would have these words on false prophets understood in general, not on some individual, following Marloratus in his commentary on this passage. But their explication is opposed to the ancient Fathers and the text itself. For these words were spoken on one Antichrist, as Chrysostom, Cyril and all the Fathers witness on this citation.[7]

Besides this, the Lord opposes himself to another man, i.e. person to person, not kingdom to kingdom or sect to sect, as is clear from the pronouns and phrases: "I," another "in my name," that is in his own name, "me," etc. Therefore, just as Christ was one and an individual man, so also Antichrist will be one and an individual man.

Next, Christ says here that Antichrist will be received

---

[6] John 5.

[7] Ambrose on 2 Thessal. 2; Jerome, *epist. Ad Algasiam*, quest. 11; Augustine, *Tract. In Joann.*, tract 29; Irenaeus, *Contra haeres.*, lib. 5; Theodoret, *in Epitome divionorum decretorum*, chapter on Antichrist, and others.

by the Jews for a Messiah. Moreover, it is certain that the Jews wait for one certain and singular man. All false prophets come not in their own name but in that of another. "Prophets that falsely prophesy in my name, these are not sent, etc."[8] But the Lord spoke about one specific man who will come in his own name, that is, who does not recognize some God, but "will extol himself," as Paul says, "over everything which is called God."

Next, many false prophets came before the coming of Christ and many were going to come after. Therefore, if he were speaking on false prophets the Lord would not have said: "If another will have come," but that many are coming.

The second passage is of Paul. "Unless first dissension will have come, and the man of sin will have been revealed, the son of perdition ... And then that wicked man will be revealed, whom the Lord Jesus will kill by the breath of his mouth."[9] Our adversaries understand these words on the true Antichrist, but the Apostle speaks on a certain specific and particular person, as is clear from the articles in the Greek: "ἀποχαλυφθη ὁ ἄνθρωποος τῆς ἁμαρτίας ὁ υἱὸς τῆς ἀπωλειας ... καὶ τότε ἀποχαλυφθήσεταὶ ὁ ἄνομος; as Epiphanius teaches, the Greek articles draw together the meaning to one certain matter, that ἄνθρωπος will mean a man in common but ὁ ἄνθρωπος an individual man.[10] It is quite the wonder, that

---

[8] Jeremiah 14:14.

[9] 2 Thessalonians 2: 3, 7-8.

[10] Translator's note: To make this clear for those who do not know Greek, the citation is the original for 2 Thessalonians, where a definite article is used for man [ἄνθρωπος]. In Greek there is a definite article before every noun; normally if it is not included, it means "a" thing instead of "the" thing, except in the case of a predicate nominative (linking verb) in what is called the attributive

none of our adversaries who boast of their expertise in language happened to notice this.

The third citation is that of 1 John 2, where we read thus: "ἠκούσατε ὅτι ὁ ἀντίχρισος ἔρκεται, καὶ νῦν ἀντίχρισοι πολλὸι γεγόνασιν." or, "You have heard that *the* Antichrist is coming, and now there are many Antichrists." There, he places an article ahead of Antichrist properly so called, but without the article it would convey the name of Antichrist received commonly, clearly indicating that Antichrist properly so called is one certain person while Antichrist commonly received is not a certain person, but every heretic in kind.

The fourth passage is from Daniel chapter 7, 11 and 12, where he speaks on Antichrist, which Jerome and Theodoret as well as other Fathers teach on this passage,[11] and even Calvin, the Centuriators, and Beza in their citations above. Moreover, in Daniel, Antichrist is not called one kingdom but one specific king from ten kings whom he will discover in the world; he will altogether abolish three from the midst and subject the other seven to himself. Add what Calvin says, that Daniel speaks literally on Antiochus Epiphanies[12] and allegorically on Antichrist whose figure was Antiochus, which Cyprian and Jerome

---

position. Therefore, by saying "the man" [ὁ ἄνθρωπος], St. Paul is identifying a specific man, not "a man" in general which he would have done by dropping the article. Lest anyone think this is a weak argument or a semantic point, in the Greek language the poets and dramatists make use of the articles for this very same purpose.

[11]   Irenaeus, lib. 5; Augustine, *de Civitate Dei*, ch. 23.

[12]   Translator's note: Antiochus IV (*Epiphanies*, i.e. the Illustrious) was the successor of Alexander the Great's empire in Syria. After losing to the Romans in a war in Egypt he retired to Syria and began the persecution of, the Jews which lead to their uprising recorded in the books of the Maccabees in the Bible.

also teach.[13] But Antiochus Epiphanius was a certain specific and singular person; therefore, Antichrist ought also to be a certain, specific person.

The fifth and last passage is in the book of the Apocalypse 13 and 17. Such passages are understood on Antichrist, as Irenaeus teaches, and it is clear from the similarity of the words to those places in Daniel and John. Each make mention of ten kings who will be on the earth when Antichrist will come and each predicts that the kingdom of Antichrist is going to endure for three and a half years. Just as Daniel speaks on one king so does John in the book of the Apocalypse.

The same is proven from the Fathers who teach in a common consensus on Antichrist. Firstly, that he will be the chosen instrument of the Devil to the extent that a plenitude of diabolic malice will inhabit him corporally, just as in Christ the man the plenitude of divinity dwelled in him corporally. Secondly, Antichrist will not reign more than three and a half years, and hence they teach Antichrist is going to be only one man.[14]

Now I shall respond to the first argument of Beza: In the time of the Apostles Antichrist began to live secretly, but not in his own person, rather in his precursors. Just as Christ began to come from the origin of the world in the patriarchs and prophets (who came before him and signified him so that it could be said the mystery of

---

[13] Cyprian, *de exhortations martyrii*, ch. 11; Jerome in Daniel 11 and 12.

[14] See Irenaeus, lib. 5 near the end. Cyril of Jerusalem, *Catechesi* 15. Chrysostom, *in 2 Thessal. 2*; Theodoret, *hist.*, ch. 11; Ambrose *in cap. 21 Lucae*; Jerome, *in cap. 7 Danielis et quaest. 11 ad Algasiam*; Augustine, *de civitate Dei*, lib. 21, for many chapters, and *in Psalm 9*; Gregory, *Moral.*, lib. 32, ch. 12; Damascene, lib. 4, ch. 28; and Hippolytus the Martyr, *in oratione de consummatione mundi*.

godliness began to operate from the beginning of the world), he did not come in his own proper person until the time when he received flesh from the Blessed Virgin Mary. In like manner, Antichrist began to come soon after Christ was assumed into heaven in his precursors, and the mystery of iniquity began to work, namely in heretics and tyrants persecuting the Church; especially in Simon Magus, who said he was Christ, and in Nero who first began to oppose the Church. Just the same, he will not come in his own person until the end of the world. Therefore, the spiritual persecution of Simon Magus and the temporal persecution of Nero is called the mystery of iniquity because they were signs and figures of the persecution of Antichrist.

That this is the true explication of the Pauline passages can be shown in two ways. Firstly, from all the interpreters of this passage. Certainly, all understood through the mystery of iniquity in Paul either the persecution of Nero, as Ambrose and Chrysostom on this citation, as well as Jerome;[15] or heretics who secretly deceive, as Theodoret and Sedulius remark on this verse along with Augustine.[16]

Secondly, from reason, taken from the admission of our adversaries who say that Antichrist is properly the seat of the Roman Pontiff.

Therefore, if Antichrist, properly so called, was born in the time of the Apostles, it follows that Peter and Paul were properly said to be Antichrists, although in secret, and Nero and Simon Magus were the true Christ. It is certain that in the time of the Apostles there were no other bishops at Rome than Peter and Paul. Irenaeus eloquently affirms that the Roman See was founded by Peter and Paul

---

[15]   *Ad Algasiam*, quaest. 11.

[16]   *De Civitate Dei*, lib. 20, ch. 19.

and that they sat there as its first bishops.[17] All the Fathers whom we cited in the last book teach the same thing. It is also certain that Simon Magus and Nero battled with the Apostles Peter and Paul.

But if this does not please our adversaries, that Peter and Paul were Antichrists and Simon and Nero the true Christ, they are compelled to affirm that Antichrist did not exist in the time of the Apostles *per se*, rather only in his specific type. The consequence of that makes Beza's point, that Antichrist could not be one man unless we would grant that he lived from the time of the Apostles even to the end of the world, utterly ridiculous.

To confirm this, I say John spoke in that mode in which the Lord spoke on Elijah: "Elijah indeed is going to come and he will restore all things but I say to you that Elijah already came, and they did not recognize him."[18] In other words, Elijah was going to come in his own person but he already came in one like him, that is John the Baptist.

Now to the Second argument. In the first place, we must deny that Daniel always understands individual kingdoms for individual beasts. For sometimes he means one kingdom for one beast, as in chapter 7 where he understands the kingdom of the Assyrians for the lion; the kingdom of the Persians for the bear; the empire of the Greeks for the leopard; and through another unnamed beast the empire of the Romans. Sometimes he understands one king, as in the eighth chapter where he understands King Darius, the last king of the Persians, through the ram and Alexander the Great through the goat. Next, the consequent of the argument is denied. For Paul understands for "the man of sin" not someone from

---

[17] Irenaeus, lib. 3, ch. 3.

[18] Matthew 17:11-12.

the four beasts described by Daniel, but that little horn which, in Daniel, prevails over the ten horns of the four beasts, i.e., that one king who rose from modest circumstances to subjugate all other kings to himself.

I respond to the final argument in several ways to show how impudent Calvin is when he writes that those who do not gather from his argument that the Roman Pontiff is the Antichrist err from their own will. Firstly, Antichrist can correctly be understood through "apostasy" in Paul's citation. Thus, the Greek interpreters understand it in a common consensus.[19] Moreover, Antichrist is called apostasy both through metonym,[20] because the case will be that many will recede from God, and through a certain excellence; there will be a characteristic apostasy that can be called apostasy itself.

Secondly, Apostasy can be taken up as the defection from the Roman Empire, as many Latins explain.[21] For as we will show in the following chapter, Antichrist will not come until the Roman Empire shall altogether fall to ruin.

Thirdly, if we were to admit that through apostasy defection from the true faith and religion of Christ is understood (as Calvin claims), still we would not be constrained by difficulties on that account. For Paul did not necessarily speak of the apostasy of many ages; he could

---

[19]   Chrysostom, Theodoret, Theophylactus and Oecumenius. Additionaly, St. Augustine in *de Civitate Dei*, lib. 20, ch. 19.

[20]   Metonym is a linguistic device in classical languages such as Greek and Latin to use a name associated with a certain subject to indicate people carried out a verb in relation to it. Common examples would be "We were busy with Mercury" which would mean we transacted business, because Mercury is the god of commerce, or in the Aeneid book 4 it speaks of the keels of the ships to mean the ships themselves. Thus calling Antichrist Apostasy is to mean there will be a great Apostasy. -Translator's note.

[21]   Ambrose, Sedulius and Primasius.

speak on a certain great and singular apostasy that will only be in that brief time in which Antichrist will reign. St. Augustine writes that he was also understood in this way by many of the Fathers, and they taught that when Antichrist appears all secret heretics or false Christians will go to him and from that event the greatest apostasy is going to occur, such as had never been before.

Fourthly, if we were to concede to Calvin that St. Paul speaks on the apostasy of many ages, he still gains nothing. Accordingly, we would be able say that apostasy does not necessarily pertain to one body and kingdom of Antichrist, nor demands one head, but is a defection to the kingdom of Antichrist that will happen in different places, under different kings and on different occasions. We now see that Africa defected to Muhammad, a great part of Asia to Nestorius and the Monophysites, and other provinces to other sects.

Fifthly and lastly, if we were to grant to Calvin a general Apostasy from the faith and that the kingdom of Antichrist endured for many years, it would not immediately follow that the Pope is Antichrist. For it still might be asked whether certain men have defected from the faith and religion of Christ; it could be us or them, that is, Catholics or Lutherans. Although they say we are the ones who have defected, nevertheless, they have not yet proved it, nor has it been declared by any common judge.

We can much more easily prove that it is the Lutherans that are the ones that defected than they can prove Catholics defected. Accordingly, they defected from the Church in which they were first and they do not even deny it. For (that I might pass over the rest), when Erasmus of Rotterdam says on that passage of 2 Thessalonians 2: "Then that wicked man will be revealed," he ingeniously confesses that nearly all the predecessors of the Lutherans and himself at one time obeyed the Roman Pontiff. Therefore, they defected from the Church and religion of their predecessors. On the other hand, they have not shown to this point that we have defected from some Church, nor could they ever show it. Therefore, since they read Paul: "Until a dissension will come, or apostasy and that wicked man will be revealed, etc.," and they know they have left the Church in which they were, while we have persevered in the same one that was always established, it is a wonder that they do not at least fear lest Paul might have spoken about them.

From this second chapter we have the second argument: to prove that the Pope is not the Antichrist. Therefore, if Antichrist is one person, yet there were and will be many Popes provided with the same dignity and power, then certainly Antichrist must be sought somewhere other than in the Roman See.

CHAPTER III

It is Shown That Antichrist has not yet Come.

ANY false suspicions and errors exist in regard to the third proposition, on the time of the coming of Antichrist both among Catholics and heretics. Yet with this distinction, Catholics know that Antichrist is not coming until the end of the world (which is true), but some err in that they think the end of the world is nearer than it really may be. On the other hand, the heretics err in the fact that they think Antichrist is coming long before the end of the world, and that he really already has come. Therefore, we shall speak on each error.

In the first place, all the Fathers who noticed the malice of their times suspected that the times of Antichrist approached. Thus the Thessalonians thought in the time of the Apostles that the day of the Lord approached, which the Apostle corrected in 2 Thessalonians 2. Likewise, St. Cyprian says: "Since Antichrist threatens, let the soldiers be prepared for battle, etc."[1] He also says in another epistle: "You ought to know, as well as believe and hold for a certain fact, that the day of persecution of the head has begun, and the end of the world and time of Antichrist approaches."[2] Jerome says: "He who held fast arises in our midst and we do not understand that Antichrist approaches?"[3] St. Gregory the Great: "All which has been

---

[1] Lib. 3, epist. 1.

[2] Lib. 4, epistle 6.

[3] *Epistola ad Ageruchiam de Monogamia.*

19

predicted comes to pass; the proud king is near."[4] Gregory also boldly pronounced the end of the world.[5] But these were suspicions, not errors, since these holy Fathers did not dare to define a certain time.

Next, others more boldly constituted a certain time. St. Jerome relates in *de illustribus viris* that in 200 A.D., a certain Jude thought Antichrist was coming and the world was ending; clearly he was deceived. Again Lactantius says: "Every expectation is no more than two hundred years, etc."[6] There he teaches that Antichrist was coming and the world was to end two hundred years from his time. He also lived in the times of Constantine, around the 300th year of Christ; so he thought the world would by chance end in the year 500; but experience shows he was also deceived.

St. Augustine relates the error of some who said that the world would end around the year 400 from the ascension of the Lord,[7] and also some who established the thousandth year. They were all deceived. It also happened even to the Pagans, who, as Augustine witnesses in the same book, gathered from I know not what divine oracle that the Christian religion would only endure for three hundred and sixty five years. There was a certain bishop, Florentinus by name, who asserted around the year 1105 that Antichrist had already been born, and hence the end of the world was closing in. The Council of Florence, having three hundred and forty bishops, was gathered for

---

[4]   Lib. 4, epistle 38.

[5]   Homil. 1 in Evangelia.

[6]   *Diviarum institutionum*, lib. 7, ch. 25.

[7]   *De Civitate Dei*, lib. 18, ch. 53.

this reason by Pope Paschal II.[8]

Next, there was also a famous opinion that had many defenders,[9] that the world was going to endure for 6,000 years, since God had created the world in six days, and a thousand years is to God one day. The writers of the Talmud also agree with this opinion, and they say that they had a vision of the Prophet Elijah in which it is asserted that the world will endure for six thousand years.

This opinion cannot yet be refuted from experience, because according to the true chronology more or less 5600 years have elapsed since the beginning of the world. Ambrose rejects this opinion, asserting in his time that six thousand years had already elapsed, though obviously he is misled.[10] The moderation of St. Augustine is the best, since he thought the opinion probable, and followed it as probable.[11] From here, it does not follow that we know the last day. Moreover, we say it is probable, that the world will not endure beyond six thousand years, but we do not say that it is certain. On that account, St. Augustine bitterly rebuked those who asserted that the world is going to end at a certain time, when the Lord said: "It is not for us to know the time and the hour which the Father has placed in his power."[12] Laying all these aside, let us come to the heretics.

All the heretics of this time teach that the Roman Pontiff is the Antichrist, and now openly lives in the world,

---

[8] See the Chronicle of Matthew Palmeri, and Platina in *vita Paschalis II.*

[9] Justin, q. 71 *ad Gentes*; Irenaeus *adv. Haer.*, lib. 5; Lactantius, lib. 7, ch. 14; Hilary on ch. 17 of St. Matthew; Jerome in Ps. 89 to Cyprian.

[10] Ambrose *in Lucam*, lib. 7, ch. 2.

[11] *De Civitate Dei*, lib. 20, ch. 7.

[12] See Augustine, Epistle 80 *ad Hesychium*, in Psalm 89, and *de Civitate Dei*, lib. 18, ch. 53.

but they do not agree among themselves on the time in which he appeared. They have six opinions.

The First are the Samosatens, who bide their time in Hungary and Transylvania. They teach in a certain book which they titled: *Premonitions of Christ and the Apostles on the abolition of Christ through Antichrist*, that a little after the times of the Apostles Antichrist appeared; that is without a doubt when it began to be preached that Christ is the eternal son of God. They think, on the other hand, that Christ is a pure man, and that there is only one person in God, and this faith was preached by Christ and the Apostles. Thus, a little after the death of the Apostles, Antichrist came to Rome and after abolishing Christ the pure man, introduced another eternal Christ, and made God triune, and Christ twofold.

This opinion is easily refuted, apart from the arguments which we asserted above against all the heretics, and in two ways. Firstly, because when Antichrist will have come, *he will make himself God*, not someone else, as the Apostle says.[13] Moreover, they themselves claim that the Roman Pontiff does not make himself God, but preached Christ and made him God from a true man. Secondly, because they say that soon after Christ and the Apostles slept, the true faith of Christ was thoroughly extinguished and the whole world began to worship Christ as God. But Christ preached that the gates of hell were not going to prevail against the Church, and the Angel Gabriel preached that the kingdom of Christ would be forever.[14] David preached that all kings would serve Christ.[15]

---

[13] 2 Thess. 2:4.

[14] Luke 1:33.

[15] Psalm 71 (72):10-11.

Therefore, how true is it that in the very beginning the nascent Church was destroyed by Antichrist?

The second opinion is of the Lutheran, Illyricus, who teaches in his Third *Catalogue* that Antichrist came when the Roman Empire fell into ruin. Moreover, it is certain that the Roman Empire began to fall after the tenth year of Honorius, when Rome was first taken, that is in the year of the Lord 412, as Blondus showed;[16] yet, Illyricus seems to understand this concerning the conception, not the birth of Antichrist. Accordingly he teaches the same thing in the *Centuries*,[17] that Antichrist was conceived in some manner at the beginning of the year 400, thereafter animated and formed in the womb of his mother, around the year 500; and at length was born in the year 606, when the Eastern Emperor Phocas conceded to the Roman Pontiff that he could be called head of the whole Church. He teaches the same thing in another place, that Antichrist was going to rule savagely with the spiritual sword for 1260 years, but with the temporal sword for 666 years, and then the end of the world would come.

The first number he gathers from Apocalypse 11, where it is said the time of Antichrist would be 1260 days. Illyricus would have it that a day is taken as a year. The second number he gathers from Apocalypse 13, where the number of the beast is 666.

This opinion can be refuted in two ways. Firstly, it follows that Antichrist was not only born but also died, and hence the end of the world already came. For the Roman Pontiff took up the temporal sword, that is temporal dominion, at least in the year 699. Then Aripertus gave to the Roman Pontiff the Coctian Alps, where Genoa

---

[16]   *Decadis Primae Historiarum*, lib. 1, ab Inclinatione Romani Imperii.

[17]   *Cent. 6*, ch. 1.

is now. Later, in the year 714, Luitprandus confirmed that donation, as Ado of Vienna and Blondus affirm, not to mention the Centuriators and Theodore Bibliander, who remarked for the year 714 that this province became the first Papist province.

Not long after, that is, in the year 760, Pepin gave the Exarchate of Ravenna to the Roman Pontiffs, along with a great part of Italy as many historians witness—even the Centuriators and Bibliander. Therefore, if Antichrist began to reign in the year 760, and endured for 666 years, then the end of the world happened in the year of Christ 1421, and now there have been more than 150 years after Antichrist died. But if the beginning of his reign is placed earlier, that is in the year 699, then the end will be placed in the year 1360 and now more than 200 years will have transpired from the death of Antichrist.

Perhaps they will respond that after the 666th year of his reign Antichrist did not die but only lost his temporal dominion. Thus, they might say that the spiritual kingdom of Antichrist endured for 1260 years, which still would not have ended, and if they were to begin from the year 666, consequently they ought to say that the spiritual kingdom of antichrist ought to endure considerably beyond his temporal kingdom. But that is certainly absurd and against all authors, and besides, it at least follows that the Popes ought to have lost their temporal dominion 200 years ago, which is opposed to the obvious fact.

Secondly, the same error can be refuted because it follows from the error of the Centuriators, who thought they discovered exactly when the world will end, which is against the words of the Lord in Acts I and Matthew 24. What should follow is clear since, if they know that Antichrist began to reign with the spiritual sword in the year 606, they know that he was going to reign only 1260 years and then the Lord is going to come to judge right after, as they gather from Paul in 2 Thessal. 2. Therefore, they know the last judgment is going to be in the year 1466. But if they do not know this, they are compelled also to not know whether Antichrist has come.

The third opinion is of David Chytraeus who teaches with Illyricus in his commentary on chapter 9 of the Apocalypse, namely that Antichrist appeared around the year of the Lord 600, and that this is sufficient to show that St. Gregory was the first Antichrist Pope. Chytraeus, however, does not agree with that which is asserted by Illyricus, insofar as the time and duration of Antichrist, but he prudently advises that it is not to be defined so boldly. He attempts to show with three reasons that Antichrist appeared in the year 600.

Firstly, because in that time Gregory established the invocation of the saints and Masses for the dead. Secondly, because in the year 606, Pope Boniface III asked the title of universal bishop from the Emperor Phocas. He adds the third reason in his commentary on chapter 13, that this time plainly and especially agrees with the number of the name of Antichrist, which contains 666 as it is contained in the Apocalypse, ch. 13.

Furthermore, Chytraeus adds that from this same number of the name Antichrist the time can be gathered wherein Pepin confirmed the reign of Antichrist. For as many years as there are from the year 97 in which John wrote the Apocalypse even to Pepin is without a doubt 666 years. Likewise, Jan Hus reckons the time from when the Roman Pontiff was declared Antichrist back to Pepin to be almost 666.

This opinion can be easily refuted, as it rests upon frauds alone. For in the first place Gregory was not the first who invoked saints and taught that Masses were to be offered up for the dead. All the Fathers taught this very thing as we showed in another place. For the present Ambrose suffices, who preceded Gregory by 200 years. He says in his book on widows: "The angels are to be observed, the martyrs prayed to."[18] He also says in his epistle to Faustus on the death of his sister: "Therefore, I deem that she is not to be wept for with tears but pursued with prayers; you ought not grieve for her but commend her soul to God with offerings."[19]

Next, Phocas did not give the title of "universal" to the Pope but addressed him as head of the churches. Even Justinian had already done the same long before, in an epistle to John II, and before that the Council of Chalcedon had done so in an epistle to Leo I. Therefore, there is simply no reason to place the coming of Antichrist in the time of the Emperor Phocas.

As to what Chytraeus adds on the number 666, it is altogether inept because that number does not agree precisely with the times that he would have it Antichrist appeared, or was confirmed, or declared to be so. For from Christ to the sanction of Phocas there are 607 years, not 666. From the revelation in the Apocalypse to Pepin 658 years, and from Pepin to Jan Hus there are, as he says, 640. But certainly John the Apostle in the Apocalypse recorded a precise number since he also adds minute details. Moreover, Jan Hus was not the first to declare that the Pope is Antichrist; Wycliff had already done that. Nay more, Jan Hus never even said that the Pope is Antichrist.

---

[18] *De Viduis.*

[19] *Lib. 2 epist. 8 ad Fuastum de obitu sororis.*

For in art. 19 of the Council of Constance, after being condemned, he says that the clergy, through their avarice, prepare the way for Antichrist. Next, all Lutherans boast that Luther was the first to unmask Antichrist, which brings us to the next opinion.

The fourth opinion is of Luther in his computation of time, where he places two arrivals of Antichrist. One, with the spiritual sword, after the year 600, when Phocas called the Roman Pontiff the head of all churches. He also says that Gregory was the last Roman Pontiff. The second is when he arrives with the temporal sword after the year 1000. Bibliander teaches the same thing.[20] Therefore, Luther and Bibliander agree in the first arrival with the Centuriators and Chytraeus—with the exception that Luther and Bibliander say that Gregory was a good and holy Pope while the Centuriators and Chytraeus say that Gregory above all did his best to introduce Antichrist and hence, he was the worst Pope, which is a horrendous blasphemy. In the second arrival, Luther and the Centuriators clearly disagree.

This opinion, apart from the common arguments which will be made afterward, is easily refuted. Luther places the arrival of Antichrist in the year 600 and 1000 altogether without reason. On the year 600 we have already spoken in refutation of Chytraeus. Concerning the year 1000, it can easily be shown, since Luther places the beginning of the temporal reign of Antichrist in that time when Pope Gregory VIII deposed the Emperor Henry IV, for then he ruled temporally as well as waged wars. Well now, all of these things already happened, as Gregory II excommunicated the [Byzantine] Emperor Leo, and deprived him of the rule of Italy in the year 715, as the historians Cedreno and Zonaras witness in the life of the

---

[20]   *Chronicum*, tab. 11 & 13. ,

same Leo. Furthermore, we already showed that the Roman Pontiffs had temporal dominion in the year 700, three hundred years before the first millennium.

Next, the Centuriators witness that Stephen III waged wars around the year 750,[21] and Adrian I could be said to have done the same thing, as well as other of their successors. In like manner, around the year 850, Leo IV, a holy man as well as famous for miracles, waged war against the Saracens. He reported a singular victory and fortified Rome with towers and ramparts still; he girded the Vatican hill with a wall, which thereafter was called after his name *civitas Leonina*, as nearly all historians of that time relate, and even the Centuriators themselves.[22]

The fifth opinion is of Henry Bullinger. In the preface to his homilies on the Apocalypse he wrote that Antichrist appeared in the year 753. Such an opinion disagrees with all those whom we cited above, and thence can easily be refuted because it rests upon a very weak foundation. Bullinger teaches in the Apocalypse, ch. 13, that the number found there of the name of the Beast, 666, means by that number the time of the arrival of Antichrist; in other words, so many years after the Apocalypse was written, Antichrist was going to come. And because it is certain from Irenaeus that the Apocalypse was written around the end of the reign of the Emperor Domitian, i.e., around the year 97, he gathers Antichrist was going to come in the year 753, by computing 666 years from the year 97.

To this point the opinion of certain Catholics can also be related, such as Jodocus Clicthovaeus, who reckoned

---

[21] *Cent. 8*, ch. 10.

[22] *Cent. 9*, ch. 10.

from the commentaries of St. John Damascene[23] that Muhammad was Antichrist properly so called because he came around the year 666 according to what John had said before. But this reasoning amounts to nothing. In the first place, the Centuriators protest and contend that the number in the book of the Apocalypse does not mean the time of the birth of Antichrist, but of his death. Moreover, John the Evangelist, in chapter 13 of the Apocalypse, rejects the commentary both of Illyricus and Bullinger, since he explains himself that the number is not of the times but the name of Antichrist; *i.e.* Antichrist is going to have a name, whose letters in Greek form the number 666, as Irenaeus and all other Fathers explain.

Besides, no change is read in the Roman Pontiffs for that year 753. Moreover, Muhammad could not come then since he was born in the year 597 and began to call himself a prophet in the year 623. Next, he died in the year 632, as Palmerius witnesses in his *Chronicle*. Therefore, he did not make it to the year 666.

The sixth opinion is of Wolfgang Musculus, who in his works under the title *de Ecclesia*,[24] affirms that Antichrist came a little after the times of St. Bernard, i.e. around the year 1200. He attempts to show this because St. Bernard enumerates many vices of men, and especially of Churchmen, and very serious persecutions of the Church, adding: "It remains only for the man of sin to be revealed."[25] But this opinion is refuted without much effort: St. Bernard merely suspected from the evils which he saw that Antichrist was near, just as we said many Fathers suspected it from their times, such as Cyprian,

---

23   St. John Damascene, *De Fide*, lib. 4, ch. 28.

24   Chapter 12.

25   Bernard, serm. 6, in Ps. 90.

Jerome and Gregory, and Bernard was deceived in that suspicion just as they. Besides, the Popes from the year 900 to 1000 were without comparison worse than the Popes from 1100 to 1200. So if the former were not Antichrist, why would the latter be?

CHAPTER IV

The First proof: the Rule of Antichrist has not yet Begun.

THEREFORE, the true opinion is that Antichrist has not yet begun to reign, nor come, rather he is going to come and rule around the end of the world. Yet, inasmuch as he has not yet come he cannot be known. This opinion destroys all those mentioned above and clearly shows that the Roman Pontiffs are not Antichrists. It is proven by six reasons.

It must be known that the Holy Spirit gave us six certain signs of the arrival of Antichrist in the Scriptures: Two preceding Antichrist, namely preaching of the Gospel and the desolation of the Roman Empire; two accompanying it, certainly the preaching of Enoch and Elijah, and a great and remarkable persecution, so much that public religion would altogether cease; two subsequent signs, namely the desolation of Antichrist after three and a half years and then the end of the world, which we see presently still exists.

Hence, the first proof is taken from the first sign preceding Antichrist. The Scriptures witness that in the whole world the Gospel must be preached before the last persecution will come, which will be roused by Antichrist: "This Gospel of the kingdom in testimony to the whole world, in witness to all the Gentiles."[1] The fact that this should happen before the arrival of Antichrist can be proved by this reason: because in the time of Antichrist the cruelty of that last persecution will impede all public

---

[1] Matthew 24:14.

exercise of the true religion.

Yet, because our adversaries do not admit this reasoning (nor is it now the time to deduce from their own principles), we will prove it from the testimonies of the Fathers. Thus Hilary explains these words of Matthew: "The Gospel of the kingdom will be preached in the whole world, and then the consummation will come." Clearly he teaches that Antichrist, which he calls the abomination of desolation, is not going to come unless the preaching of the Gospel will precede him throughout the whole world.

St. Cyril, Theodoret, and St. John Damascene teach the same thing with eloquent words,[2] and besides, the same is gathered from the text because the Gospel says that before that greatest and last tribulation shall come, the Gospel must be preached such as it was not before nor will be afterward. The Fathers and above all, St. Augustine, teach that the persecution of Antichrist is meant by such a tribulation.[3] Yet the Gospel was not preached in the whole world in the time that the new Samosatens say Antichrist came, that is around the year 200 or 300. It is clear from Origen, who asserted at that time the Gospel was not yet preached everywhere.[4] Likewise from Ruffinus, who witnesses that in the time of Constantine the Emperor, that is, after the year 300, that the Gospel was preached in the furthest parts of India, since before they had never heard anything about Christ.[5] Next, we learn it from St. Augustine who says with some experience one would find that there were many nations in his time that had not yet

---

[2]   Cyril of Jerusalem, *Catechesi 15*; Theodoret in 2 Thessal. 2; Damascene *de fide*, lib. 4, ch. 28; as well as many others.

[3]   *De Civitate Dei*, lib. 20, ch. 8 & 19.

[4]   Origen, *homil. 28 in Matthaeum.*

[5]   Ruffinus, *Hist.*, lib.. 10, ch. 9.

heard anything about Christ.[6]

Now, it is clear that the preaching of the Gospel was not completed around the year 600 or 700, in which the Centuriators, Chytraeus, Luther and Bullinger place the arrival of Antichrist. This is so from the conversion of the Vandals, the Poles, the Moravians and similar nations, who it is certain had not heard the preaching of the Gospel until after the year 800, as the Centuriators themselves affirm in their histories.[7] Likewise, the preaching of the Gospel had not been completed in the times of St. Bernard, where Wolfgang Musculus places the arrival of Antichrist. This is clear from Bernard himself, who asserts in book 3 of *de Consideratione* that still in his time there were nations who had not heard the Gospel.

Next, experience teaches that even in our time the Gospel has not been preached in the whole world. Very vast regions were discovered in both the East and West in which no memory of the Gospel exists. Nor can it be said the faith was ever there but later extinguished, for at least some vestige would remain, either there or in the writings of the Fathers. Besides, we know where all the Apostles preached and the places were marked by many, though I would not say by all; but the new world was recently discovered; it was not known in Apostolic times or any other until a little before our age.

Only one objection can be made against this proof: That perhaps Scripture, when it says the Gospel must be preached in the whole world, does not speak absolutely but rather receives the whole for a part by a figure of speech, just as Luke 2 when it is said: "An edict went out from Caesar Augustus that the whole world should be enrolled."

---

[6] Epistle 80.

[7] *Cent. 9*, ch. 2, col. 15 & 18.; *Cent 10*, ch. 2, column 18 & 19.

Otherwise what Paul says would be false, that already in his time: "The sound of the Apostles has gone out through all the earth,"[8] as well as what he says in Colossians: "The truth of the Gospel which has arrived even to you, just as it bears fruit and increases in the whole world... which has been preached to every creature which is under heaven."[9]

I respond: Without a doubt it is not through a figure that the Gospel ought to be preached and churches constituted, but properly and absolutely in the whole world, that is in every nation. In the first place, St. Augustine expressly teaches this,[10] as well as the other fathers we have cited, such as Origen and Jerome in their commentaries on Matthew 24.

Next, it can be proved by three reasons. 1) Christ said preaching in the whole world is a sign of the consummation of the age. Therefore, he adds: "And then the consummation will come." But if this is not properly, but synecdochically that the Gospel ought to be preached in the whole world, it avails to nothing as a sign. For in the first 20 years the Gospel was preached by the Apostles in the whole world. 2) Secondly, as Augustine reasons, all nations were properly promised to Christ; "All nations will serve him."[11] Christ generally died for all and as a result (as related in Apocalypse 7), the elect will be described as being from all nations, peoples, tribes and tongues. Therefore, even preaching properly ought to be general. For that reason, in Matthew 24 it is said that the Gospel must be preached in the whole world, "in testimony to all nations;" that is, lest any nation could be excused in the

---

[8]　Romans 10:15.

[9]　Collosians 1: 6.

[10]　Epistle 80 to Hesychius.

[11]　Psalm. 71 (72):11.

day of judgment for its infidelity on account of ignorance. So, before the general judgment, general preaching ought to precede.

Augustine responds to those passages of Paul in Epistle 80, and says that Paul, when he spoke in Romans 10, received the past for the future, just as David did who uses the same words. Moreover, when he says in Colosians: "The Gospel is in the whole world," he did not wish to say it was in act but in potency, because without a doubt the seed of the Divine Word was thrown out by the Apostles in the whole world, so that little by little in bearing fruit and increasing it was going to fill the whole world. Just in the same way that someone could suppose the flame from different parts of the city could truly be said to burn the whole of that city because the fire was applied little by little by burning and was going to take up the whole city; this is the same thing the Apostle indicates when he says: "In the whole world it is bearing fruit and increasing." Therefore, it did not plainly overtake the whole world since still it had to be propagated, but still has seized it in some way—that is, in potency not in act.

A response can be made with Jerome and St. Thomas that the Gospel arrived to the nations in two ways: in one way through report; in another through proper preachers and the foundation of churches. Indeed, in the first manner the Gospel arrived to all the Nations of the whole world then known in the time of the Apostles and in this way Paul could speak. Chrysostom should also be understood in the same way on Matthew 24. In the second manner it could not have arrived then but was going to in its own time, and on this the Lord speaks in Matthew 24 as well as in the last Chapter of Luke and Acts 1.

3) Lastly, add that it is not absurd were we to concede the Lord spoke properly but the Apostle figuratively,

whereby we would be compelled to take the words of the Lord in their own meaning; they do not have the same force if they were to be accommodated to the words of St. Paul, especially when the Lord spoke on the future, while Paul spoke on the past.

CHAPTER V

The Second Proof: Desolation of the Roman Empire

HE SECOND proof is taken from another sign that will precede the times of Antichrist, which will be the *desolation* in every way possible of the Roman Empire. At length, it must be known that the Roman Empire was divided into ten kings, none of whom will be called "King of the Romans," although all will occupy some provinces of the Roman Empire in the same way that the King of France, the King of Spain, the Queen of England and by chance some others hold parts of the Roman Empire; at length they are not Roman kings or emperors, but until they cease to hold those dominions Antichrist cannot come.[1]

Irenaeus[2] proves this from Daniel, chapters 2 and 7, as well as from chapter 17 of the Apocalypse. In Daniel there is a description of particular kingdoms even to the end of the world, and a certain one is described whose golden head signifies the first kingdom, that is, of the Assyrians; its silver chest is the second kingdom, that is of Persia; the bronze mid-section is the third kingdom, that is of the Hellenistic Empires; the iron legs represent the fourth kingdom, that is of Rome. Now Rome was divided into two

---

[1] Although this is an attempt to interpret prophecy on Bellarmine's part combined with history it is not, strictly speaking, impossible even after the revolutions of the 18th and 19th century as there are still kings over England, the Netherlands, Spain and a few other areas once controlled by the Romans.
-Translator's note.

[2] *Adv. Haere.*, lib. 5.

parts for a very long time, just as there are two legs and they are the longest part of the body. Next, ten toes arose from the two legs, and with these the whole statue ended; certainly this means that the Roman Empire was divided into ten kings, none of whom will be king of the Romans, just as no toe is the leg. But now, in chapter 7, Daniel clearly marks out through the four beasts the same four kingdoms which mean the last ten kings who will arise from the Roman Empire, yet they will not be Roman emperors; just as the horns begin from the beast but are not the beast itself.

Next, John describes a beast with seven heads and ten horns, upon which a certain woman sat, and explains the woman is a great city which sits upon seven hills, that is Rome;[3] the seven heads are those seven mountains, and also the seven kings, by which number all the Roman emperors are understood. He says the ten horns are ten kings that will rule together at one time, and lest we think these by chance will be Roman kings, he adds that these kings will hate the harlot and will make desolation, because they will so divide the Roman Empire among themselves that they will almost destroy it.

Next, Paul proves the same thing in 2 Thessal. 2:6 when he says: "And now you know what withholds, that he may be revealed in his time. For the mystery of iniquity already works, only that he who now holds should hold until he be taken out of the way. And then that wicked one will be revealed, etc." There, Paul does not dare to write openly on the toppling of the Roman Empire, because he still explained openly in the presence of Romans and he spoke as if to say: You know what should impede the arrival of Antichrist. I said to you, the Roman Empire impedes it, because its sins have not been filled and Antichrist, who

---

[3] Apocalypse 17: 1-5.

shall abolish this empire on account of its sins, will not yet have come. Therefore, the one who now holds the Roman Empire should hold it, that is, he will rule, until it comes to pass from our midst, that is, it shall be abolished; then the wicked one will be revealed. The Greek and Latin Fathers explain it alike. Cyril of Jerusalem teaches on this passage: "The aforesaid Antichrist will come when the times of the Roman Empire have been completed."[4] St. John Chrysostom explains: "When the Roman Empire has been abolished from our midst, then Antichrist will come." Theophylactus and Oecumenius teach similar things.

From the Latins. Tertullian says that Christians prayed for the Roman Empire to long endure, because they know that when the Empire has been overturned, the supreme destruction of the world threatens.[5] Lactantius, explaining the signs which precede Antichrist and the end of the world, says: "The Roman name, which now rules the world (the soul shudders to say it, but I will speak on what is going to come), will be abolished from earth, and the Empire overturned in Asia, and again the East will rule and the West will serve it."[6] St. Ambrose, speaking on 2 Thess., says that Antichrist is going to come after the disappearance of the Roman Empire.

St. Jerome, explaining the same citation of St. Paul, says: "Christ will not come unless first there will be such a dissension that all the nations which now are subject to the Roman Empire will recede from it and unless the Roman Empire will already have been made desolate and thus Antichrist precede him."[7] Next, St. Augustine explains

---

4   *Catechesis* 15.

5   *Apologeticus*, ch. 32.

6   Lib. 7, ch. 15.

7   Quaest. 11 ad Algasiam.

on this citation: "Such a one who merely commands, let him command, until he shall be taken from the midst; that is, abolished, and then the wicked one will be revealed, whom no one questions means Antichrist."[8]

But this sign was not fulfilled in those times in which the Transylvanian Anti-Trinitarians say Antichrist came, that is, around the year 200, because then the Roman Empire particularly flourished and would do so long after.

But it is clear that this sign has never been fulfilled even to this point, because the succession still remains, and the name Roman Emperor—even by a wondrous providence of God seeing that the Empire failed in the west, which is one of the legs of the statue of Daniel—remained unharmed in the East, the other leg. But because the Empire of the East was to be destroyed by the Turks (and now we see this has come to pass), again God erected in the West the other leg, that is, the Western Empire through Charlemagne, and that emperor still endures.

Moreover, the fact that Rome itself, according to the prophecy of John, would fall in a certain measure, and lose the Empire, does not impede us. For the Roman Empire can stand well without the city of Rome, and the Roman Emperor can be so called when he lacks Rome, in the manner that he succeeds another Roman Emperor in the same dignity and power, whether he should have more or fewer provinces in his Empire. Otherwise Valens, Arcadius, Theodosius the younger, or their other successors even to Justinian, who all lacked Rome, could not be called Roman Emperors. Nor even would Charlemagne and his successors, who also did not possess the city of Rome, ever have been Emperors, which is false, and that is clear for two reasons.

---

[8] *De Civitate Dei*, lib.. 20, ch. 19.

First, by this reason alone the emperor, who now is, precedes all Christian kings, even if they are otherwise greater and more powerful than he is. Next, because it is certain that Charlemagne was created emperor with the agreement of the Romans, as Paul the Deacon witnesses;[9] and by the Greek emperor himself through legates sent to greet the emperor, as Ado witnesses,[10] as well as by the Persians and Arabs, that the emperor should be adorned with gifts, as Otho of Frisia relates.[11] Next, the Lutherans boast that they have three prince electors of the Roman Empire. Hence they cannot deny that the Roman Empire still endures.[12]

Orosius rightly compares the Empire of Babylon with Rome, and he says that God by far more agreeably managed things with the Romans than with the Babylonians. For after 1,064 years from which Babylon was founded, in one day Babylon, the head of the Empire, was taken, and the emperor killed, and the empire was destroyed and desolate. But after so many years, 1,064 from which Rome began, Rome was taken by the Goths; but the Emperor Honorius, who then ruled, was unharmed, and the Roman Empire was preserved.

Hence the deception of our adversaries appears. They think the decay of the Roman Empire suffices for the

---

[9] *Rerum Romanarum*, lib. 23.

[10] Chronicum, for the year 810.

[11] *Hist.*, lib. 5, ch. 31.

[12] In this place it is worth noting that Greek Orthodox apologists often reject this and claim Charlemagne usurped the title. Modern research, however, bears out what Bellarmine is saying. Dimitri Vasilev, in his work *The Byzantine Empire*, notes that Charlemagne had proposed marriage to the Empress Irene and was honored by her and a subsequent emperor who acknowledged him as Emperor of the West. -Translator's note.

coming of Antichrist; but Paul, John and Daniel, as well as the Fathers we mentioned above did not say that decay was necessary, but desolation.

On the other hand, Luther, Illyricus and David Chytraeus object that this proof rather more makes their case, for it was preached by John in the Apocalypse, chapter 13, that the beast, which signifies the Roman Empire, was to be wounded to death, and was again healed by Antichrist. This certainly came about when the Pope restored again the Western Empire, which had already perished, in conferring upon Charlemagne the title and dignity of Emperor. Therefore, it is clearly understood from this translation or restoration of the Empire that the Roman Pope is truly the Antichrist.[13] Illyricus confirms this argument from Ambrose, who, while explaining the words of St. Paul, says that Antichrist is going to return freedom to the Romans, but under his own name. The Pope seems to have done this when he created an emperor for the Romans, who still depended upon him.

I respond: we read nowhere in John that when the beast is going to be healed by Antichrist that it signified the Roman Empire. But we read this, that one of the heads of the beast will die, and a little after is going to rise again, by the works of the dragon, that is the devil; which nearly all the Fathers explain concerns Antichrist himself, who makes himself dead, and again by some diabolic craft he himself raises himself, that he would imitate the true death and resurrection of Christ, and in that manner will seduce many.

St. Gregory so explains this, as do Primasius, Bede, Haymo, Anselm, Richardus and Rupertus on chapter 13 of the Apocalypse. And the text itself compels us that

---

[13] See Illyricus, *Contra primatum Papae*; *Centur. 8*, ch. 10, col. 751; Chytraeum, *in Apocalyps.*, ch. 13.

through the head of the beast, which was dead and brought back to life, we should not understand Charlemagne, but Antichrist. Accordingly, that head, as John writes, had power only for 42 months, and blasphemed God and those who dwelled in heaven, and commanded in every tribe and people, tongue, nation, and all who dwelled on earth adored it but of such things we do not read on Charlemagne or any of his successors. Furthermore, Charlemagne ruled for more than 42 months and he did not blaspheme God and the saints, but rather more wonderfully venerated them, and many of his successors imitated his piety.

Next, neither Charlemagne himself, nor his successors, held power over every tribe, people, tongue and nation, as is known by all. Hence St. Ambrose did not speak on what the Pope did when he said a new Roman Empire that was to be created by Antichrist; rather after the Roman Empire had been overturned freedom was to be restored to the Romans, which it is not read the Pope ever did.

CHAPTER VI
A Third Proof: Enoch and Elijah

A THIRD proof is taken from the arrival of Enoch and Elijah, who are still living and do so for the purpose that they might oppose the arrival of Antichrist, preserve the elect in the faith of Christ and finally convert the Jews; it is certain that this still has not been fulfilled. There are four Scriptures on this matter. The first, from Malachi 4: "Behold, I will send the Prophet Elijah to you, before the great day of the Lord will come, and convert the hearts of the fathers toward the sons, and the hearts of the sons to their fathers." The second, from Eccles. 68, where we read on Elijah: "You who were received in a fiery whirlwind, in the whirlwind of vast horses. You who are inscribed in the judgments of the times, appease the anger of the Lord, reconcile the heart of the father to the son, and restore the tribe of Jacob." And in chapter 64: "Enoch pleased God, and was lifted up into paradise, that he should bring repentance to the nations." Third, from Matthew 17: "Elijah is going to come, and will restore all things." Fourth, from the Apocalypse 11: "I will give my two witnesses, and they will prophecy for 1,260 days."

Even Theodore Bibliander relates all these citations in his *Chronicle*, but he says through Enoch and Elijah all the faithful ministers are understood, whom God rouses in the time of Antichrist; such were Luther, Zwingli and the others. At length, he concludes: "This is why it is a puerile imagination, or a Jewish dream, to await either Elijah or Enoch as definite persons in their properties." Chytraeus teaches the same thing in his commentary on that citation of the Apocalypse. And they attempt to show that the Lord

45

taught that those passages in Malachi which speak about Elijah must be understood on John the Baptist: "He is Elijah who is going to come." And St. Jerome, in chapter 4 of Malachi, shows this to be about all the choir of prophets, that is on the doctrine of all the prophets.

Now, it does not seem to be a puerile imagination to us but a very true teaching, that Enoch and Elijah are going to come in their own persons—and the contrary is either heresy or an error proximate to heresy. Firstly, it is proved from those four Scriptures, since it is obvious that the words of Malachi could not be understood concerning anything at all, such as on teachers, like Luther and Zwingli and similar things, for Malachi says that the Jews must be converted by Elijah, and that they must be sent especially on account of the Jews which we see in that verse: "I will send to you," and in Sirach: "... to restore the tribe of Jacob." Yet, Luther and Zwingli have converted none of the Jews.

Moreover, it is certain that these cannot be understood on John the Baptist to the letter, but only on Elijah. We know that Malachi speaks on the second coming of the Lord because it will be to judge. For he says: "Before the great and terrible day of the Lord should come." The first coming is not called the great and terrible, but the acceptable time, and the day of salvation. For that reason it is added: "Lest by chance coming I shall strike the earth with a curse;" in other words, lest coming to judgment and discovering all the wicked, I shall condemn the whole world. Therefore, I shall send Elijah, that I should have others whom I shall save. But in the first coming the Lord did not come to judge, but to be judged; not to destroy, but to save.

I will respond a little later to the words of Matthew 11. Now I speak to Jerome; in his commentary on Malachi he also did not think that Malachi spoke about Elijah, but in his commentary on Matthew 11 and 17 he thought and taught the contrary. Next, this is the common interpretation of the faithful, as St. Augustine witnesses.[1]

Moreover, Sirach speaks on the very persons of Enoch and Elijah, not on others. It is proven because Sirach says about this Enoch, "He who was taken into paradise [is going to come] that he should give punishment to the nations." Also this Elijah, who was taken up in a chariot of fiery horses was going to come to restore the tribes of Israel. Certainly, such verses do not fit, unless they are about these particular persons.

I cannot marvel enough at what comes to mind from bishop Jansenius on this passage. He wrote on it that although it was the opinion of the Fathers that Elijah himself was going to come, still he is not convinced from this passage, for it can be said that the author of Sirach wrote that according to the received opinion of his time, wherein it was believed from the words of Malachi that Elijah was truly going to come in his person before the Messiah; although this would not be fulfilled in his own person, but in the one who was going to come in the spirit and power of Elijah. Yet, if that is so, as Jansenius says, it follows that Sirach erred, and wrote falsely. Rather, unless I am mistaken, Jansenius changed his opinion; writing on chapter 17 of Matthew he teaches that the passage of Malachi cannot be understood literally except concerning the true Elijah, which likewise would compel him to say the same on the verse in Sirach, which he expressed with no doubt on Malachi.

Now that the words of the Lord in Matthew 17 are understood on the true Elijah, not on John, is clear because John had already come and run his course, and still the

---

[1] *De civit. Dei,* lib. 20, cap 29.

Lord said: "Elijah is going to come." Moreover, it can be proved that all the Doctors only understand this to be on the true Elijah. Firstly, because the Apostles who advanced the question on Elijah were Peter, James and John, and they took up the occasion from the transfiguration of the Lord, where they saw Moses and Elijah. Therefore, when they ask: "What about what the scribes say, that Elijah must come first?" they spoke on that Elijah whom they saw on the mountain with Christ. Therefore, when Christ responded, "Indeed, Elijah is going to come and he will restore all things," he also spoke on that particular Elijah who had appeared in the transfiguration. Secondly, the same is clear from the words themselves: "And he will restore all things." Truly, John the Baptist did not do that, nor anyone else. For to restore all things is to recall all Jews, heretics and perhaps many Catholics deceived by Antichrist to the true faith.

But Bibliander insists that the Lord speaks of John the Baptist in Matthew 11: "He is Elijah who is going to come," that is, he [John] is the Elijah promised by Malachi. I respond: The Lord wanted to say that John was the promised Elijah, not literally, but allegorically. Therefore, he sent him ahead, although you wish to receive him, as if to say, indeed the Elijah promised in his person is going to come in the last coming. Still, if you also wish to receive some Elijah in the first coming, then receive John. For that reason he also added: "He who has ears to hear, let him hear," thereby showing it was a mystery that he had said John was Elijah.

Next, that the words of John in Apocalypse 11 should be understood on the individual persons of Enoch and Elijah is clear not from all the doctors but for the very reason that John says in the same place that they will be killed by Antichrist and that their bodies will remain

unburied on a street in Jerusalem, and after three days they
will rise again, and they will ascend into heaven. No one
has yet done that.

Still, David Chytraeus tries to respond in a commentary
on this citation. He says first: John wanted to signify the
many Lutheran ministers that would be killed by Papists,
to whom God at length restored to life although he
brought them into heaven, they were going to live forever.
Secondly, he adds a little below that after the ministers
were killed, life of the body was to be restored on the last
day of resurrection. Thirdly, he adds in the same place that
it can even signify through this restoration of life, and that
we shall see many other ministers with the same zeal and
power raised by God.

Yet these are very weak responses. The first cannot be
defended, because the beatitude of the soul is not the
restoration of lost life, but the acquisition of new life. Next,
these two witnesses in the Apocalypse will rise in the sight
of all and with their bodies restored; turning they will be
lifted up, which certainly is not fulfilled in the beatitude of
the soul. The second answer avails to nothing since John
says that those two witnesses were going to rise before the
last day, while the state of this world still endures. But
John adds that it is to strike great fear to their enemies by
their resurrection, and a little afterward the movement of
the world is going to happen, and seven thousand men are
going to perish. Next, the third answer is not to the point.
For the Scripture says that those same who were dead are
to be roused to life, and taken up into heaven. Moreover,
we have not yet seen any Lutheran minister resurrect, or
be assumed into heaven. Why, John says that Enoch and
Elijah are going to preach wearing sackcloth, and the
Lutherans so hate sackcloth that if by chance Enoch and
Elijah wear it while they are Lutherans, they will

immediately be cast out.

Secondly, it is proved from the consensus of the Fathers that Enoch and Elijah are truly going to come in their persons in the time of Antichrist. For Hilary, Jerome, Origen, Chrysostom and all other interpreters of Matthew 17 assert this about Elijah. In like manner do Lactantius,[2] Theodoret,[3] as well as Augustine[4] and Primasius.[5]

On Enoch together with Elijah, many who write on the Apocalypse assert that they are going to come to oppose Antichrist, such as Bede, Richard, and Arethas. Arethas also adds that it is believed without exception by the whole Church. Moreover, John Damascene,[6] Hippolytus[7] the martyr, St. Gregory the Great[8] and Augustine[9] teach the same.

Thirdly it is proved because otherwise no reason can be given why these two should be taken up before death, and still live in mortal flesh who are going to die someday. Albeit the Jews say, as Rabi Salomon,[10] that Enoch was killed by God before his time, because he was light and inconstant, and they assert that Elijah, when he was born in the fiery chariot, was burned in his whole body by the flame. Perhaps the Lutherans who deny they are coming back think likewise; still all Catholics hold with certain faith that both live in their bodies. For the Apostle teaches

---

[2] Lib. 7, cap. 17.

[3] In cap. ult Malachiae.

[4] Tracta. 4 in Ioannem.

[5] In cap. 11 Apocalypsis.

[6] Lib. 4, capite 28.

[7] In oratione de mundi consummatione.

[8] Moralium, lib. 21 36 & lib. 9 cap. 4.

[9] Genes. ad litteram, lib. 9, cap. 6.

[10] In cap. 5 Genes.

that Enoch has not yet died;[11] Enoch was borne up lest he would see death, and that both he and Elijah were not yet dead but were going to die. Apart from those cited above, Irenaeus, Tertullian, Jerome, Augustine and Epiphanius clearly teach this.

Irenaeus, speaking abut Enoch and Elijah, says: "The priests who are disciples of the apostles say that those, who were borne up thence (into early Paradise) were borne up and there remain even to the end, tasting incorruption."[12] Tertullian says about Enoch: "He has not yet tasted death, as glittering in eternity."[13] Epiphanius says about Enoch and Elijah: "These two remain in body and soul on account of hope."[14] Jerome in an epistle to Pammachius against John of Jerusalem says: "Enoch was borne up in the flesh; Elijah still was taken up in the flesh into heaven, and still has not yet died, being a tenant of Paradise, etc." Augustine says: "We do not doubt that Enoch and Elijah live in the bodies in which they were born."[15]

---

[11] Hebrews 11:5.

[12] Lib. 5.

[13] *Contra Iudaeos*, cap 1 de Henoch.

[14] In Ancorato.

[15] *De peccato Originali*, cap. 23.

CHAPTER VII
The Fourth Proof: the Persecution of Antichrist

THE FOURTH proof is taken from the fact that it is certain the persecution of Antichrist will be the most severe ever known, to the extent that all public ceremonies and sacrifices of religion will cease. We still do not see any of that. Now, the fact that the last persecution is going to be very severe is clear from what we read in Matthew 24: "Then there will be a great tribulation, such as has not been from the beginning of the world, nor will be." Moreover, we read in Apocalypse 20: "Then Satan must be loosed," who was bound even to that time.

St. Augustine, disputing on this citation, says in the time of Antichrist the Devil will be loosed, and hence that persecution will be much more severe than all the ones that preceded it;[1] the Devil can rage so much more cruelly loosed than bound. Therefore, he says, then the Devil is going plague the Church with all his own and their strength. Further, Hippolytus the martyr and St. Cyril say that the martyrs whom Antichrist will kill are going to be more illustrious than all the previous ones, because the old martyrs fought against the human ministers of the devil, but these will fight against the Devil himself prowling personally. But certainly we have experienced nothing like that from the year 600 or even 1000.

The heretics say that they suffer a great persecution from Antichrist because some of their number are burned. But what comparison is there of that sort of persecution

---

[1] *De Civitate Dei*, lib. 20, ch. 8&9.

with that carried out by Nero, Domitian, Decius, Diocletian, and others? Accordingly, for one heretic who is burned, a thousand Christians formerly were burned—and that was exercised in the whole Roman world, not only in one place. Furthermore, at present when the supreme penalty is given a man is merely burned, but in ancient times they exercised the most diverse and unbelievable torments.[2]

Pope Damasus writes in the life of Marcellinus that over seventeen thousand Christians were killed by Diocletian, and Eusebius, who lived at that time, writes that all the prisons were so full with martyrs that no place was left for criminals.[3] Moreover, in the whole of the book we cited, so many crowns were conferred for martyrdom in two hundred years that it would be impossible to undertake their number. Besides, the fact is that the heretics killed many more Catholics in the last ten or fifteen years in France and Flanders than inquisitors burned heretics in perhaps the last hundred. Therefore, they cannot call this persecution, but rather more civil war. For as Augustine teaches, when the true persecution of Antichrist will come, tribulation will only be upon the sons of the Church, but not upon their persecutors just as in the time of Diocletian and the princes of this world, Christians alone were slaughtered, but they did not slaughter.

For all that, were this to be called a persecution, then Catholics have a better claim to have suffered it than the Lutherans and Calvinists. For Catholics are the ones who were cast out from many areas and lost their churches, patrimony and even their country, without a doubt, to invaders seizing their things for the Ministers of this new

---

[2] From the pagan side, see Cornelius Tacitus on Nero, and from our side Eusebius in his *Ecclesiastical History*.

[3] Eusebius, *Ecclesiastical History*, lib. 8 cap. 6.

Gospel; and as we said from the commentary of Laurence Surius and other historians of this time, it can be recognized that the fury of the Calvinists has taken up many more Catholics in a few years than heretics by the judgment of Catholic princes were given punishment for the denial of faith.

Nevertheless, Augustine proves the fact that the persecution is going to be well-known and manifest, while commenting on those words of Apocalypse 20: "And they surrounded the camp of the saints, and the beloved city."[4] By these words, it is meant that all the wicked were going to be together in the army of Antichrist, and were going to assault every church of the saints in open battle. For now there are many false men in the Church, who, concealing their malice, are outside the Church in heart but within the body. St. Augustine says: "But then they will all break out in open persecution from their hiding places of hate." Certainly, this has not yet been fulfilled in our time even though there never was a greater number of false brethren and feigned Christians. That this persecution is neither known nor manifested, neither they who say they suffer nor we who are alleged to cause it can say when this will begin.

Without a doubt the persecutions of Nero, Domitian and of other Roman Emperors were recorded diligently by Eusebius, Orosius, and Sulpitius. Nobody questions when these persecutions began and when they ended, just as no one questions when Christ came, because it was true and manifest and we absolutely know when it was and by whom it was made manifest. Nor are there any opinions on our side on the matter. But the heretics who say that Antichrist has come and now for so many years has exercised persecution still cannot advance one author who

---

[4] *De Civitate Dei*, lib. 20, cap. 11.

recorded when Antichrist came or to whom he appeared first, or when he began the persecution. They even disagree among themselves, so much so that one might say he came in the year 200, another in the year 666, while another in 1273. Another yet will say the year 1000, while another 1200, so they do not speak as men who are awake, but seem like men who dream in quiet.

Next, the fact that in the time of Antichrist, on account of the atrocity of persecution, the public office and daily sacrifice of the Church will cease, which Daniel clearly teaches: "From the time when the continual sacrifice will have been taken away for 1290 days." In that place, by the consensus of every writer, he speaks on the time of Antichrist. Furthermore, Irenaeus, Jerome, Theodoret, Hippolytus the martyr and Primasius all express the same thing, that Antichrist is going to forbid all divine worship which is now exercised in the churches of Christians, especially the most holy sacrifice of the Eucharist. That this sign has not yet been fulfilled is evident from experience.

From that we can gather three things. 1) Antichrist has not yet come, since the continual sacrifice is still in force. 2) The Roman Pontiff is not the antichrist, rather, he is quite contrary to him, since the Pope carefully honors and guards the sacrifice which Antichrist is going to take away. 3) The heretics of this time, apart from all other things, are precursors of Antichrist since no one more ardently desires to altogether abolish the sacrifice of the Eucharist than they.

CHAPTER VIII
The Fifth Proof: the Duration of Antichrist

HE FIFTH proof is taken from the duration of Antichrist. Antichrist will not reign more than three and a half years, yet now the Pope has reigned spiritually over the Church for more than 1500 years. Further, not one of them can be assigned that will have reigned precisely three and a half years so as to be accounted for Antichrist. Therefore, not only is the Pope not the Antichrist, but the latter has not yet come.

Now, that the reign of Antichrist is going to be for three and a half years is gathered from Daniel[1] and from the Apocalypse.[2] There we read that the reign of Antichrist is going to endure through time, times and half a time. For time is understood as one year, through times two years, through half a time, half a year. John argues this same thing, for in Apocalypse 11 and 13, he says Antichrist is going to reign for 42 months, which correctly corresponds to three and a half years. The Hebrews use years and lunar months, even if they reconcile them to the solar by adding one lunar cycle to the sixth year. Moreover, three and a half lunar years correctly makes 42 months, or 1260 days; correspondingly the lunar year is full and complete in 12 months, of which each has 30 days, as Augustine teaches.[3]

What Daniel 12 says, namely that Antichrist is going to reign for 1290 days is not opposed to us, even though it is

---

[1] Daniel 7:25 and 12:11-12.

[2] Apocalypse 12:6.

[3] *De Civitate Dei*, lib. 15, cap. 14.

30 more days than John had said. This is because John
speaks on Enoch and Elijah, who will be slain by Antichrist
a month before Antichrist shall perish.

Our adversaries respond to this in three ways. First,
Chytraeus[4] says that times (*tempora*) cannot be taken for
three and a half years because it is opposed to experience;
and Paul says Antichrist is going to endure even to the
coming of Christ.[5]

Secondly, he says a certain time can be placed for an
uncertain one; hence, more than a thousand years ought to
be understood for 42 months or 1260 days. Bullinger says
the same thing,[6] and his reason seems to be the one which
Luther insinuates in his supposition of the times; because
without a doubt it is certain from Apocalypse 20 that the
Devil will be loosed for a thousand years. Thus, the coming
of Antichrist with the temporal sword was in the
thousandth year from Christ and he has already reigned
more than 500 years; therefore, it is fitting to receive those
42 months as an uncertain time.

Thirdly, the Centuriators respond that Daniel and John
take a day for a year, and hence for 1260 days, 1260 years
should be understood.[7] The reason can be that in Daniel 9,
70 weeks are understood to be 700 years, not days. And
Ezechiel 4 says: "I gave you a day for a year." And Luke 13:
"Today it is fitting for me to walk, and tomorrow as well as
every day;" that is, to live for three years. Chytraeus puts
this reasoning in chapter 11 of the Apocalypse, where he
says the years and months of the same are called angelic
years and months, not human.

---

4   *In cap. 11 & 13 Apocalypsis.*

5   2 Thess. 2:6.

6   *Sermon* 46 in Apocalypsim.

7   *Cent.* I, lib. 2, cap. 4, col. 438.

Now, the common opinion of the Fathers is to the contrary. Let us look at those who assert that Antichrist will only reign for three and a half years due to the passages we have noted. Hippolytus the martyr, in his *Oration on the Consummation of the World*, says: "Antichrist will reign over the earth for three and a half years, afterward his kingdom and glory will be snatched away from him." Irenaeus said: "He will reign for three years and six months, then the Lord will come from heaven."[8] Jerome adds: "The time means a year; the times, according to the propriety of the Hebrew terminology, which has dual numbers, prefigures two years; half of the time, six months, in which the saints must be entrusted to the power of Antichrist."[9] St. Cyril said: "Antichrist will reign for merely three and a half years which we say not from some Apocryphal book, but from Daniel the Prophet."[10] Likewise St. Augustine said: "Even a man who is half asleep and reads these things can hardly doubt that reign of Antichrist against the Church will be very savage, although it is to last a scanty space of time. For time and times, and half a season is one year and two, and half which makes three years and a half; and through this, the number of days that were placed in the Scripture makes clear the number of months."[11] Theodoret says like things on chapter 8 of Daniel, as do Primasius, Bede, Anselm, Haymo, Arethas, Richard and Rupert on the Apocalypse.

Secondly, the same is proven from the fact that the Scriptures say that the time in which the Devil is unleashed, as well as of Antichrist, will be very brief. "Woe

---

[8]   Lib. 5, towards the end.

[9]   *In Danielis*, cap. 7.

[10]   *Catechesis*, 25.

[11]   *De Civitate Dei*, lib. 20, cap. 23.

to the earth and sea, because the devil descends to you having great wrath, knowing that he has but a short time."[12] And again: "He bound him for a thousand years, and after these he ought to be freed for a short time."[13] How I ask, will this be true, if Antichrist will reign for 1270 years? For he will be free longer than he was bound.

Thirdly, because, as Augustine[14] and Gregory the Great[15] argue, unless that fearsome persecution were brief, many would perish who are not going to perish. This is why the Lord also says: "Unless those days would be brief, all flesh would not be saved."[16]

Fourthly, Christ preached for only three and a half years. Therefore, it would be fitting that Antichrist is not permitted to preach longer.

Fifth, the sum of those 1260 years, which our adversaries constitute, can in no way be accommodated to those words of Daniel and of John: "Time, times and half a time." For through time it ought to be understood without a doubt one certain number like one day, one week, one month, one year, one purification,[17] one jubilee,[18] one century, one millennium. But if we receive one millennium, then Antichrist will reign for 3500 years, which our adversaries do not admit. If we receive one

---

[12] Apocalypse 12:12.

[13] Apocalypse 20:3.

[14] *De Civitate Dei*, lib. 20.

[15] *Morales* lib. 33, cap. 12.

[16] Matthew 24:22.

[17] Translator's note: The Romans had a purifying ceremony every 5 years (*lustrum*) and the word was used as a term for a period of 5 years.

[18] Translator's note: In the Old Testament, a Shemita (*Jubilaeus*) or Jubilee was every 50 years, and here would be used to denote a 50 year period.

century, then the time of Antichrist will be 350 years, which they also do not admit, and the same is clear concerning one jubilee, etc.

Sixth, when we read Daniel 4, we read that the number of times that will pass are seven in which Nebuchadnezzar will be going to be outside his kingdom, but for those times all understand seven years. If we would understand years of years, as our adversaries would have it in their treatment of Antichrist, it would behoove them to say that Nebuchadnezzar lived outside his kingdom for 2,555 years.

It is not difficult to answer their petty syllogisms. For when Chytraeus said that what Daniel and John spoke of cannot be received as three and a half years, nor properly for our usage of years, because experience witnesses that Antichrist has already been prowling for a longer time, he manifestly begs the question, as the logicians say. For he assumes what is in question. That very thing is asked, whether Antichrist has come. But when he adds that by the opinion of St. Paul, Antichrist was going to rule even to the second coming of Christ, and concludes that he must reign longer than three and a half years, he does not see that he either again begs the question or says nothing. For no order can be made, unless it is assumed that Antichrist has already come—but that is what the very question is about.

But to that which both he and Henry Bullinger say, that a certain number is taken up for an uncertain period in this passage, I respond: a certain number is only placed for an uncertain one when some full and perfect number is placed, such as ten, a hundred, or a thousand, but not when different numbers are assigned where great and small are mixed. Then, a certain number must be taken up for an uncertain one, just as when the Scripture says in Apocalypse 20 that the devil was bound for a thousand years, as Sts. Augustine and Gregory say,[19] but not when it assigns time, times and half time, or 1260 days, or 42 months. For to what end are there a variety of numbers, if an uncertain time is meant?

Now I will address the argument of Illyricus. In the Scripture one does discover what can rightly be called weeks of years. Still, not days for years, or months for years. For weeks of years we read in Leviticus 25: "You will count for yourself seven weeks of years, etc." And certainly it is right to say that week is counted by the number seven in Greek, Latin and Hebrew. In Hebrew they say שָׁבוּעַ (sha-bo-ach, seventh) from שָׁבַע (sha-bach), which is seven, as is also said in Greek by ἑϐδομὰς, and in Latin by *septimana*, through a number containing seven; just as seven days are called a week of days, so seven years are a week of years. But month of years, or day for year we never read, nor would it be correct to say it, because a month is not counted by some number, but by the cycle of the moon, which finished in thirty days. Hence the Hebrews call month יֶרַח (ya-rech), that is moon, or חֹדֶשׁ (ko-desh); that is the beginning of the moon, and in Greek month is μήν because moon is called μήνη.

In like manner, day does not mean a number, but a time of light, as in Genesis: "God called the light day, and the darkness night." Nor is the passage of Ezechiel opposed to this: "I give to you a day for a year."[20] There, he did not wish to say years are literally meant by days, otherwise it would behoove Ezechiel to have slept on his left side for 390 years, which is impossible. For God had commanded that he should sleep upon his left for 390 days and added: "I give to you a day for a year." So if those days were

---

[19] *Loc. Cit.*

[20] Ezechiel 4:5.

received for years, Ezechiel ought to sleep on his side for 390 years. Yet he did not live that long. Therefore, it must be said that in that passage a day is truly received for days, but can mean years through a type, because those 390 days in which Ezechiel slept were a sign of the sleep of God, through which he tolerated the sins of the Israelites for 390 years.

Now, to the objection made by Chytraeus from Luke 13: "It is fitting for me to walk today and tomorrow, as well as the day after," I respond: When Christ said this, he did not mean by these words that he was still going to preach for three years since the Lord said this in the last year of his life. For as Jerome notes,[21] the matter speaks for itself. Matthew, Mark and Luke did not write the deeds and words of the first two years of Christ's public ministry, rather only the third year. Therefore, the Lord either understood by those three days the triduum which was about to be taken up on the journey to Jerusalem (as St. Albert and Cajetan explain), or he certainly wished to show by that manner of speaking that he was going to remain and preach still a little while, as Jansenius rightly teaches. Lastly, where in the world did Illyricus and Chytraeus find days and angelic months? None are found in Scripture.

---

[21] Liber *de Scriptoribus Ecclesiasticis*, in Ioanne.

CHAPTER IX
The Sixth Proof: the End of the World

HE SIXTH proof is taken from the last sign following Antichrist, that the end of the world will come about. For the arrival of Antichrist will be a little before the end of the world. Therefore, if Antichrist would have come a long time ago, as our adversaries say, the world should have ended a long time ago. Daniel spoke twice about Antichrist,[1] once explaining the vision, adding each in turn; the second, that after Antichrist the last judgment immediately follows. "I considered the horns and behold, a little horn arose, and three from the first horns were torn from his face. I watched until thrones were placed, and the Ancient of Days sat, etc." And later, explaining the vision: "The fourth beast will be the fourth kingdom; the ten horns mean there will be ten kings and another kingdom will rise after them, and it will be more powerful than the first, and it will lay low the three kings ... And they will be betrayed into his hand through time, times and half a time, and he will sit in judgment, etc."

The prophecy of John is similar: "After these it will be fitting for him to be freed for a short time, and I have seen the seats, and they sat upon them and gave judgment upon them, etc."[2] Daniel said the same thing again afterward, in chapter 12. The reign of Antichrist will endure for 1,290 days, and he adds: "Blessed is he who waits and attains even to 1,335 days;" this is, even to sixty days after the

---

[1] Daniel 7:20-22; 23-27.

[2] Apocalypse 20:3-4.

death of Antichrist, because then the Lord will come to judge and he will render the crowns of justice upon the victors, just as Jerome and Theodoret show in their commentary on this citation.

Next, the same is gathered from Matthew 24: "This Gospel of the kingdom will be preached to all nations throughout the whole world, and then will come the consummation;" that is, the end of the world will be a little after. Then: "But immediately after the tribulation of those days the sun will be darkened, and the moon will not give its light; and then will appear the sign of the Son of Man, etc." St. Paul says the same thing: "Then that wicked man will be revealed, whom the Lord Jesus will kill with the breath of his mouth, and by the glory of his coming he will bring him to ruin, etc."[3] The Apostle teaches that almost immediately after Antichrist, Christ is going to come because he will intervene in that very short time, so that the frauds and deceits of Antichrist, which will have begun to be destroyed by Elijah and Enoch, will be utterly destroyed by the very arrival of Christ as well as the horrible preceding signs.

Moreover, the same is seen in 1 John 2: "Little children, now is the last hour; and just as you heard that Antichrist has come, now there are many Antichrists, whence you know it is the last hour." In other words, John says that this time from Christ even to the end of the world is the last hour, that is, the last time or the last age, as St. Augustine says. And he proves this most beautifully from this principle that we know Antichrist is going to come at the end of the world. But now we have already spoken of his many forerunners, or lesser Antichrists. The sign is certain; this is the last hour, or age. It is in the same way that one could so argue about the last hour of night for we

---

[3]   2 Thessalonians 2:8.

know the sun is going to rise at the end of the night. Furthermore, we see now many of its rays already illumine the sky so we know this is the last hour of the night.

Next, this is also the common consensus of the Fathers: Irenaeus,[4] Tertullian,[5] Augustine[6] and many others; we even see it in the testimony of our adversaries. They affirm that Antichrist is going to reign even to the end of the world, hence a little after his ruin it is going to be the end of the world. So from this sign, joined with that above, we make an unanswerable proof whereby it is proven both that Antichrist has not yet come and he is not the Roman Pontiff. For if the world is going to end immediately after the death of Antichrist and Antichrist will not be alive three and a half years after he appears, then it is clear that he will not appear or begin to reign except for three and a half years before the end of the world. But the Pope now, according to our adversaries, has reigned with both swords for more than five hundred years but still the world still endures.

---

[4] Lib. 5.

[5] *De Resurrectione.*

[6] *De Civitate Dei,* lib. 20, cap. 19.

ר 200	λ 30	τ 300
	α 1	ε 5
ו 6	τ 300	ι 10
מ 40	ε 5	τ 50
י 10	ι 10	α 1
	ν 50	ν 50
י 10	ο 70	666
ת 400	ς 200	
666	666	

This opinion is completely careless. In the first place, Irenaeus indeed says that the name λατεῖνος can probably be accommodated to Antichrist; but he adds it is much more probable that the name of Antichrist is not λατεινος, but τειταν, which also expresses that number, and the name is much more clear since it means the light of the sun.

Besides, the conjecture of Irenaeus, which was something at that time, is nothing now. For he says it is probable that Antichrist will be called Latinum, not because he ruled in Latium, but because the Latins then ruled so extensively and held almost the whole world. Since Antichrist ought to be a very powerful king, without a doubt he will seize the most powerful kingdoms that he will discover. Moreover, Irenaeus says that the kingdom of the Latins is the most powerful, since they really ruled then. Certainly that conjecture avails to nothing in our times, for the Latins no longer rule throughout the world; instead the Turks really rule, and among us the Spanish and the French, not the Latins.

Besides the name *Latin*, that it would mean Rome, is not written for ει, but through the simple Iota; and thence it does not render that number. In the same way the comment can be refuted on the word רומיית. For Roman can not end in a ת (tav), since it would be a masculine noun. For that ending is feminine in Hebrew. Without that letter ת, the number 400 is missing for the name of Antichrist. Moreover, the noun λατεῖνος, if it will be the name of Antichrist, will be proper to him especially in use, just as Arethas teaches, because it will need to be shown in a sign by all who buy or sell; yet the name λατεῖνος is common. Still, no Pope has ever been called Latinus either for their own name or for the name they take up; the Popes never call themselves Latins, only bishops or Popes.

Next, Romanus was a proper name of only one Pontiff, though still he could not be Antichrist since he did not live more than 4 months. Secondly, such a name is common.

Next, if only this name λατεῖνος or Romanus would effect the number 666, our adversaries would have an argument. But innumerable names are discovered that render the same number. Hippolytus the Martyr, in his sermon on the consummation of the world, recorded another name which renders that number, ἀρνοῦμαι; that is *I refuse*. Arethas records seven: λαμπέτης, that is *renowned*; τειτὰν, that is *the sun;* ὀνικητὴς, that is *victor;* κακὸς ὁ δηγὸς, that is *wicked general;* ἀληθὴς βλαβερὸς, that is *truly wounding;* πάλαι βάσκανος, that is *once hating;* ἀμνὸς ἄδικος, which is a Gothic name, and in Latin comes out to DCLXVI, which makes 666 if we receive a D in Latin for 500, C for one hundred, L for fifty, X for ten, V for five, and I for one.

From more recent writers William Lindanus remarks that Martin Luther rendered the number 666 if Latin letters would be received for numbers after the customary usage of Greek and Hebrew in this way: A,1; D, 2; C 3; D, 4; E5, F, 6; G, 7; H 8; I, 9; K, 10; L, 20; M, 30; N, 40; O, 50; P, 60; Q, 70; R, 80; S, 90; T, 100; V, 200; X, 300; Y, 400; Z, 500. Gilbert

Genebrardus remarks in the last book of his *Chronology* that even the name of Luther in Hebrew makes the number לולתֿר (Luliter).

I add two other things for the sake of Luther and Chytraeus, namely that דביד כיתריו, (David Chytraeus), and σαξόνειος, (the Saxon) render 666, and the latter agrees with Luther just as the name Latin does to the Pope.

ד	4	σ	200
ב	2	α	1
י	10	ξ	60
ד	4	ο	70
כ	20	ν	50
י	10	ε	5
ת	400	ι	10
ר	200	ο	70
י	10	ς	200
ו	6		
	666		666

The third opinion is of many Catholics who suspect Antichrist will be called ἄντεμος, both because this name properly agrees with him and also that it renders the number exactly, as Primasius, Anselm and Richardus argue.

This opinion is correctly refuted by Rupert, since the name which John insinuates will not be the name imposed on Antichrist by his opponents, but the name which he will take unto himself and boast in, so much so that he will command it be written on the foreheads of men. Moreover, it is not believable that he is going to take a name so odious and vile, such as ἄντεμος, and being mindful of all others noted above.

The fourth opinion is of the same Rupert, who believes

this number does not mean the name of Antichrist but means the threefold prevarication carried out by the devil in Antichrist. For a series of 6 numbers, because it does not reach as far as the sevens, in which there is rest and beatitude, is the number of the creature perishing through prevarication from rest. But the devil incurs a threefold prevarication, or rather more, he makes one threefold. First he transgressed when he sinned in himself; next, when he made the first man sin he added 60 to a simple six; then thirdly he will transgress when he will seduce the whole world through Antichrist, and then will have added 600 to 60.

The fifth opinion is of Bede, who proceeds on a contrary path, and teaches the number six is perfect, because God created the heaven and the earth in six days. Sixty, then, is more perfect and six hundred the most perfect, from which he gathers that Antichrist is meant by the number 666 because he will usurp for himself the most perfect tribute which should be given to God alone. We read a figure of it in the Book of Kings, where a weight of gold, which is offered to Solomon each year, was six hundred and sixty six thousand talents.[5] These two opinions do not appear to sufficiently square with what John says, since that number is the number of a name, not a dignity or a prevarication. Yet these Fathers would hold their opinions on this passage with as much suspicion and conjecture.

Therefore, the truest opinion of this matter is of those who confess their ignorance and say that they still do not know the name of Antichrist. Such an opinion is of Irenaeus,[6] Aerthas and others on this place of the

---

[5]   3 Kings (1 Kings) 10:14.

[6]   Lib. 5, cap. 30, 3.

Apocalypse. If I may, I will ascribe the words of Irenaeus, because Chytraeus exhorts his readers to do the same, saying:

Being zealous I exhort you that you view the last pages of Irenaeus on this place of the Apocalypse, 333 and 334, which profitably and piously dispute on this number, and among the rest he judges that Latin or Roman is the name of Antichrist, that is λατεῖνος, etc. Now Irenaeus says the following: "It is more certain and less hazardous to await the fulfillment of the prophecy than to be making surmises and casting about for any names that may present themselves, inasmuch as many names can be found possessing the number mentioned and the same question will, after all, remain unsolved. For if there are many names found possessing this number, it will be asked which among them shall the man bear when he comes. It is not through a want of names containing the number of that name that I say this, but on account of the fear of God, and zeal for the truth. For the name εὐάνθας contains the required number, but I make no claim regarding it. Then also *Lateinos* has the number six hundred and sixty-six; and it is very probable, this being the name of the last kingdom [seen by Daniel]. For the Latins are they who at present bear rule. I will not, however, make any boast over this. *Teitan* too, the first two syllables being the Greek vowels ε and ι, among all names which are found among us, is rather worthy of belief.... Inasmuch, then, as this name "Titan" has such arguments to recommend it, that from among the many names we could gather lest perhaps he who is to come will be called "Titan", it has the greatest appearance of truth. We will not, however, risk the matter nor pronounce in earnest that Antichrist is going to have this name, knowing that if it were necessary for his name to be publicly revealed at the present, the one who beheld the vision of the Apocalypse would have made it known.

So, let Chytraeus hear the profitable, pious and erudite difference of Irenaeus, and not falsely impute to him what he never said. For Irenaeus judged that Antichrist might be Latin, or Roman, but he says that as often as it was repeated, the name of Antichrist could not be known in this time, and he proved this opinion with two reasons. First, because many names are discovered which make that number, nor is it permitted to divine the name from so many like it, because it happens that it will be one which has been predicted. Next, because if God wanted it known in this time, he would have brought this out through John himself. But he adds, that it is not due to any poverty of names, but from fear of God and zeal for truth. And for that reason he brings forth three names, εὐάνθας, λατεῖνος, and ταιτᾶν, whereby the second has a greater appearance of truth than the first, and he affirms the third to have more than the second, while he avows none of them for certain.

We could add a third reason from the same passage of Irenaeus. A little before we disputed against those who were gathering false names of Antichrist for their own purpose. For this reason, he says they fall into many troubles. For they express themselves with the danger of erring and deceiving others, and also of effecting that both they and many others will quite easily be seduced by Antichrist. When he will come, he will have some name which they will persuade him to have; he will not be held by them as Antichrist, and so he will not shun it. All such dangers without a doubt come upon the Lutherans, and especially this last one, because they have persuaded themselves that the Roman Pontiff is the Antichrist. When the true Antichrist arrives they will not easily recognize it and hence, will not avoid him.

Here we must remark that when he will have come, the name of Antichrist will be well known. Before Christ came, the Jews did not know for certain by what name he would be called, although the prophets preached much concerning his name. Even one of the Sibyls, in the first book of the songs of Sibyls, remarked that the number of the name of Christ was going to be 888, even as John writes that Antichrist's number is 666. But after Christ came, all controversy was abolished, and everyone knows he is called Jesus.

"But," says the Sibyll, "I will teach you what his number may be. For eight monads there are as many tens over it. And also 8 groups of ten, will mean faithless. But you bear in mind that is the name for the human race."	I 10 η 8 σ 200 ο 70 υ 400 ς 200 888

"But," says the Sibyll, "I
will teach you what his
number may be.
For eight monads there are
as many tens over it.
And also 8 groups of ten,
will mean faithless.
But you bear in mind that
is the name for the human
race."

I 10
η 8
σ 200
ο 70
υ 400
ς 200
    888

It happens, that it is common to all prophecies of the prophets to be ambiguous and obscure until they are fulfilled, just as Irenaeus rightly teaches and proves.[7]

From these we take up the unanswerable argument to prove the Roman Pontiff is not the Antichrist and that Antichrist himself has not yet come. If Antichrist would have come and was the Roman Pontiff, his name would established for certain, as predicted by John, just as Christ for us —now there is no question—not even amongst the Turks, Jews, and Pagans, to the extent that he is named. But on the name of Antichrist there is still a great controversy, we make it plain by so many opinions that

---

[7] Irenaeus, lib. 4, cap. 43.

have been recited and refuted. Thus, the prophecy of John has not yet been fulfilled. Hence, Antichrist has not yet come nor is he the Roman Pontiff. Add the confirmation from the *Confession* of Augustine Marloratus, who in a great explication gathered from various Lutherans and Calvinists on the New Testament, so writes on this citation: "There are nearly so many explications of this passage whereby it appears it is very obscure and enigmatic." Yet if the prophecy is still very obscure and enigmatic, then it is not fulfilled; Antichrist has not come. Accordingly, all prophecies, when they are fulfilled are made evident. Therefore, why does Marloratus, lay down in his preface in the Apocalypse that it is so clear that the Roman Pontiff is the Antichrist, that if you were silent, the very stones would cry out?

CHAPTER XI
On the Mark of Antichrist.

NDEED, there are also two or three opinions on the mark of Antichrist. Firstly, the heretics of this time teach that the mark of Antichrist is some sign of obedience and union with the Roman Pontiff, yet they do not explain in the same way what that sign will be. Henry Bullinger would have it that it is the anointing of Confirmation, in which all Christians are marked on their forehead as obedient to the Roman Pontiff.[1] Theodore Bibliander says the character of Antichrist is the profession of the Roman faith, because a true worshiper would not be considered a true Christian unless he professed that he adheres to the Roman Church.[2] Additionally, David Chytraeus adds the oath of fidelity, which many are compelled to furnish to the Roman Pontiff. In like manner the priestly anointing that they receive on their forehead and hand, saying: "He impresses, as the Papists call it, an indelible character." Therefore, he sinks down to statues and consecrated bread, as well as to be present at funeral masses. Now, what Sebastian Meyer and others along with Augustine Marloratus teach on this citation of the Apocalypse are not much different. But these petty arguments are easy to refute, both because they do not agree with the words of the text itself and also because all these signs were in the Catholic Church before their opinion holds Antichrist appeared.

---

[1]   Serm. 61, *in Apocalypsim.*

[2]   *Chronicus,* tab. 10.

1) We have from the text that there is going to be one mark, not many. For Scripture always speaks on an individual number both for a mark and for the name and number of the name of Antichrist. Therefore, the mark will be one. Likewise the proper name of Antichrist and his number are one. Hence, when our adversaries multiply so many marks they show that they do not know what it is that John is speaking about.

2) That mark will be common to all men in the reign of Antichrist and such is plain from the words themselves. He will make all the small and the great, rich and poor, free and slave receive his mark. But the oath of obedience and the priestly anointing agree with a very few individuals.

3) Scripture shows that the mark is of a type that could be borne without distinction on the right hand or on the forehead. He says: "He will make all receive the mark on the right hand or on their forehead." Moreover, this agrees with none of the arguments which our adversaries advance because the anointing of chrism cannot be received in the right hand and the profession of the Roman Faith can not be received in the hand nor on the forehead; it is made by the mouth through profession and preserved in the heart by faith. The oath of fidelity is furnished by hand and mouth but in no way can it be borne on the forehead. Priestly anointing is received neither in the right hand properly, nor on the forehead, but above the crown and on the fingers of each hand. Then the last point, to be present at funeral masses and to kneel before statues and the Eucharist, are not obligations for the forehead or the hand, but rather of the whole body, and they are particularly felt in the knees.

4) The same Scripture says that in the reign of Antichrist, nobody will be allowed to buy or sell unless they show the mark, or the name, or the number of his

name. But how many people buy and sell in the dominion of the Roman Pontiff who have not yet been anointed with chrism, nor furnished an oath of fidelity and are not priests? Are there not in Rome itself, where the Roman Pontiff has his seat, a great many Jews who publicly conduct business, buying and selling, yet none of them have these signs?

Let us come to the another account, whereby we prove all of these signs are older than Antichrist. Antichrist, in the opinion of our adversaries, did not come before the year 666. Yet Tertullian flourished around the year 200 and still called Chrism (Confirmation) to mind. He says: "The flesh is washed so that the soul will be cleansed, the flesh is anointed so that the soul consecrated."[3] Cyprian lived around the year 250, and he remembered the chrism: "It is necessary for anyone who has been baptized to be anointed, so that after he has received the chrism, that is, anointing, he may be able to be the anointed of God and have in himself the grace of Christ."[4] Augustine lived around the year 420, yet he says on John: "What is it that all believers know to be the sign of Christ, but the cross? What sign is it that is applied to the forehead of believers, or in the water, by which we are regenerated, or in the oil in which we are anointed with chrism, or the sacrifice whereby we are nourished, but the cross? Without it, none of these can be done rightly."[5]

For equal reason, to adhere to the Roman Church before the year 600 was a sign and mark of a truly Catholic man. Augustine writes about Cecilianus, who lived around the year 300: "He paid no attention to the multitude of his

---

[3] *De Resurrectione Carnis.*

[4] Lib. 1, epist. 12.

[5] *Tractatus in Joannem*, 118.

conspiring enemies since he saw himself through communicatory letters joined to the Roman Church, wherein the supremacy of the Apostolic See always flourishes, and with the rest of the world, whence the Gospel came into Africa."[6] Ambrose, who lived around 390, said: "It was inquired of the bishop whether he thought with Catholic bishops, that is, whether he thought with the Roman Church."[7]

Victor of Utica, who lived around the year 490, writes of an Arian priest that wished to persuade the king not to kill a certain Catholic man using these words: "If you destroy him with a sword, the Romans will preach that he is a martyr."[8] In such a place, by the name of Romans he means African Catholics, for certainly the Arians would not speak on behalf of a Roman unless he meant the faith of the Roman Church, since they did not follow the Arian treachery.

The oath of obedience made to the Roman Pontiff is found in the time of St. Gregory,[9] and hence is before the year 606, since St. Gregory did not survive to that year.

On priestly anointing we have the testimony of Gregory Nazianzen, who lived around 380. In his *Apologetic* to his father when he became bishop of Sasimi he said: "When the anointing and the Spirit came over me, again I fell weeping and sad." There he calls to mind two anointings, one which he had received when created a priest, the other which he had to receive in the episcopal ordination. Speaking about Basil, who, after he was created a bishop refused a province, he said: "When he believed

6 Epistola 162.

7 *De obitu Satyri.*

8 *De Persecutione Wandalica*, lib. 1.

9 Lib. 10, epist. 31.

the Spirit and the business of the talents and the care of the flock was consigned to him, and he was anointed by the oil of priesthood and perfection, still he delayed to receive a prefecture from his own wisdom."

Now on the sacrifice for the dead, it will be enough to cite the testimony of Augustine, who says that it was a doctrine of the heretic Aërius that it was not fitting to offer sacrifice for the dead.[10]

Concerning the adoration of images, one testimony of Jerome, who lived in the year 400, will suffice for us. He said, in the life of Paul: "He worshiped, prostrate before the cross, just as if he discerned the Lord hanging there." Next, in the adoration of the Eucharist, St. Ambrose should be sufficient testimony. While explaining that verse: *adorate scabellum pedum eius*, he said: "Therefore, through a footstool the earth is understood; for the earth, the flesh of Christ, which today also we adore in the mysteries and which the Apostles adored in the Lord Jesus, as we said above."[11] Augustine says nearly the same thing in the same words in his explication of Psalm 98 (99).

So, since all these things which our adversaries suggest are marks of Antichrist were in the use of the Catholic Church for many years before Antichrist would have been born by their reckoning, necessarily it must be that Antichrist either learned from the Church, and so to say this is to confuse Antichrist with Christ; or none of these pertain to the marks of Antichrist. Now follows what we contend. These suffice for that rash and absurd opinion of our adversaries, which they try to show with no witnesses and no proofs.

The second opinion is of some Catholics, who think the

---

[10]   *De Haeres.*, cap. 53.

[11]   *De Spiritu Sancto*, lib. 3, cap. 12.

mark of Antichrist is a letter wherein the name of Antichrist will be written. So say Primasius, Bede and Rupert, who seem to have been deceived from something which they read: "Unless someone will have the mark of the name of the beast, or the number of his name." But John does not say this, rather he said: "Unless one will have the mark, or the name of the beast, or the number of his name." The Greek text agrees: εἰ μὴ ὁ ἔχων τὸ κάραγμα τὸ ὄνομα τοῦ θηρίου ἢ τὸν ἀριθμὸν τοῦ ὀνόματος αὐτοῦ.[12]

The third opinion is of the martyr Hippolytus, and of certain others. He thought that the mark of the beast was going to be that he would not use the sign of the cross, but rather would curse and abolish it. In this the Calvinists would be outstanding precursors of Antichrist. At any rate, I believe it is a positive character that will be devised by Antichrist, just as Christ had the sign of the cross made known to all. Yet no one will know what this character will be until Antichrist comes, just as we said on his name.

<hr />

[12] Apocalypse 13:17. Translator's note: We have revised the Greek text Bellarmine made use of ere found) with the 1904 Nestle-Aland.

CHAPTER XII
On the Begetting of Antichrist

N the fifth, concerning the begetting of Antichrist, there are some things that are clearly erroneous asserted by some individuals, then some things that are probable, and others that have been investigated and are certain. Firstly, there were once many errors on Antichrist. The first error is that Antichrist was going to be born from a virgin by a work of the devil, exactly how Christ was born by a work of the Holy Spirit.

An author of a little work on the Antichrist relates this error, which is held under the name of Augustine in the end of volume IX (though it is probable that the work is of a rabbi, certainly it cannot be of Augustine). It is clearly erroneous, for to produce a man without the male seed is a work of God alone, who can supply all efficient causes, because he alone is of infinite power and contains every perfection of creatures in his essence. The devil, however, is a creature, certainly he can do wondrous works by applying active things to passive things in a short period; but he cannot supply the active power of a cause. For this reason St. Augustine says that to be born of a virgin was such a miracle in Christ, that greater things could not be expected from God.[1]

Still it would not be an error if someone would say that Antichrist was going to be born from the devil and a woman, the same way that certain people relate that men are born from liaisons with demons. Although the devil by

---

[1] Epist. 3 *ad Volusianum.*

himself cannot produce a man without the male seed, still he can exercise a carnal act with a man taking on the form of a woman, and take his seed; and then exercise a like act with a woman in the form of a man, and place the seed received from the man into the womb of the woman to beget a man in that manner. St. Augustine witnesses this,[2] and adds that experience has so proven it that it seemed to him that one would be impudent to deny it.

The second error was of the blessed martyr Hippolytus, who in his sermon on the end of the world, teaches that Antichrist is the devil himself, who will assume false flesh from a false virgin. For as the Word of God, which is truth itself, assumed true flesh from a true virgin, so Hippolytus thought it probable that the devil, who is the father of lies, was going to simulate that he had taken human flesh from a virgin. This opinion is refuted, both because in 2 Thessalonians 2 Antichrist is called a man, and also because the rest of the Fathers write in a common consensus that Antichrist is going to be a true man.

The third error is that Antichrist is going to be a true man, but at the same time also the devil, through the incarnation of the devil, just as Christ through the Incarnation is true God and man. Several Fathers relate and refute this error.[3]

Origen believed this opinion is possible, inasmuch as he asserted that some angels were truly incarnate, which Jerome refutes in his preface to Malachi as well as in the first chapter of Haggai. And without a doubt, it is erroneous since a person cannot be created and thus sustain two finite natures in the way that the Word of God, who is infinite, can. There is no controversy on this

---

[2] *De Civitate Dei*, lib. 15, cap. 23.

[3] Jerome, *in Daniel.*, cap. 7; Bede, *in Apocal.*, cap. 13; Damascene, lib. 4, cap. 28.

amongst theologians, although some may teach that it altogether implies contradiction others teach it does not imply one. Nevertheless, all agree on the point that creatures, such as the devil, cannot do that by their power alone.

The fourth error is that Nero is going to rise from the dead and he is going to be the Antichrist, or certainly that he will still live and be preserved secretly in the vigor of youthful age and appear as he did in his own time. Sulpitius suggests this error;[4] but St. Martin writes that Nero himself will not be Antichrist, rather he is going to come with Antichrist and at length, must be destroyed by Antichrist.[5] Yet, because all these are said without any proof from reason, St. Augustine rightly calls this opinion a remarkable presumption.[6]

Apart from these errors there are two probable opinions of the holy Fathers on the begetting of Antichrist.

1) That Antichrist is going to be born from a woman by fornication, not from a legitimate marriage. St. John Damascene teaches this,[7] as well as certain others. Still, since it cannot be shown from the Scriptures it is not certain, although it is probable.

2) Antichrist will be born from the tribe of Dan, which many Fathers and Doctors assert.[8] They prove this from

---

[4] *Sacrae Historiae*, lib. 2.

[5] *Dialogus de virtutibus*, lib. 2.

[6] *De Civitate Dei*, lib. 20, cap. 19.

[7] Lib. 4, cap. 28.

[8] Irenaeus lib. 5; Hippolytus *in oratione de mundi consummatione.*; Ambrose, *de Benedictionibus Patriarcharum*, cap. 7; Augustine *in Iosue*, quaest. 22; Prosper of Aquitane *de promissionibus et praedictionibus Dei*, pars 4; Theodoret, *in Genesin.*, quest. 109; Gregory *Moralium*, lib. 31, cap. 18; Bede, Rupert, and Anselm, *in Apocal.*, cap. 7.

Genesis 49: "Let Dan be a snake on the path, let him be a horned snake on the path, etc." Likewise in Jeremiah 8: "From Dan we heard the growling of his horses, etc." Next, because in Apocalypse 7, where twelve thousand from every tribe of the sons of Israel is signified by the angel, the tribe of Dan is left out, which appears to be done in hatred of Antichrist.

This opinion is exceedingly probable on account of the authority of such Fathers; still it is not altogether certain, both because a great many of these Fathers do not say they know this but hint that it is probable, and because none of those passages of the Scripture clearly prove it. In the first place, in Genesis, Jacob seems literally to speak about Samson, when he says: "Let Dan be a serpent on the way, a horned snake on the path, and let him bite the hoofs of the horses so that the rider falls upon his back." For Samson was from the tribe of Dan, and was truly a serpent in the road for the Philistines. For he resists and plagues them everywhere. Jerome shows this in *Hebrew Questions*. It appears well enough that Jacob prayed well for his son when he said this, and hence did not predict evil but good.

Nevertheless, if this were to be accommodated to Antichrist allegorically, such as is brought in from the spiritual senses of Scripture, the argument could not be said to be more than probable. Moreover, Jeremiah 8 without a doubt does not speak on Antichrist, nor on the tribe of Dan, but Nebuchadnezzar, who was going to come to destroy Jerusalem through the region which was called Dan.[9] But why Dan, whose tribe was one of the greatest, is omitted in Apocalypse 7 is not sufficiently established.

Apart from these two probable opinions, there are two certain ones.

1) Antichrist will come particularly on account of the

---

[9]   Jerome, *in Hieremia.*

Jews, and will be received by them as if he were a Messiah;

2) He is going to be born from the nation and race of the Jews, be circumcised, and shall observe the Sabbath, at least for a time.

The first opinion is certain from the following. It is in John's Gospel where the Lord says to the Jews: "I have come in my Father's name, and you have not received me. If another will have come in my name, you will receive him." We proved that this citation ought to be understood to be about Antichrist in the second chapter above. Then, from the Apostle: "For the reason, since they do not receive the charity of truth that they may be saved, God will send to them the operation of error, that they would believe lies, etc."[10] Calvin and other heretics in commentaries on these words argue that these words are about us [Catholics], who, because we do not receive their Gospel, he permitted to be seduced by Antichrist. But we have all the interpreters on our side, who show it speaks about the Jews. See Ambrose, Chrysostom, Theodoret, Theophylactus, and Oecumenius.

Apart from them, Jerome says the following: "Antichrist will make all these things not with virtue, but from the concession of God on account of the Jews and because they refused to receive the charity of truth, the spirit of God through Christ, that having received the Savior they would be saved; God will send upon them not an operator, but the operation itself, that means the font of error, that they would believe lies, etc."[11] Even without so many commentaries of the Fathers the matter speaks for itself; the Apostle speaks about the Jews. For he says Antichrist must be sent to them who refuse to receive

---

[10] 2 Thessal. 2:10-12.

[11] Quaest. 11, ad Algasiam.

Christ. Moreover, who else is there that can be said to ought to have received Christ, but refused, more than the Jews? It also must be remarked, the Apostle did not say because they will not receive the truth but because they have not received it. Therefore, he speaks on those who refused to believe the preaching of Christ and the Apostles. It is certain in the times of the Apostles, the Gentiles eagerly received the Gospel, but the Jews refused to.

So apart from Jerome and other citations, all the other Fathers teach the same thing.[12] Even reason argues for it. For Antichrist, without a doubt, will join himself to those who are prepared to receive him; the Jews are of this sort, who await the Messiah as a temporal king and Antichrist will be such a king. For the Gentiles await no one. Moreover, Christians indeed wait upon Antichrist, but with fear and terror, not with joy and desire. Therefore, just as Christ first came to the Jews to whom he had been promised and by whom he had been awaited, and at length also joined the nations to himself, so also Antichrist will first come to the Jews, by whom he is awaited, and thereupon little by little subjugate all the nations to himself.

Now to the second opinion, that Antichrist is going to be a Jew and circumcised; this is certain and is deduced from the aforesaid. For the Jews have never received a non-Jewish man, or an uncircumcised one for a Messiah. Nay more, the Jews also await a Messiah from the family of David and the tribe of Judah; certainly Antichrist,

---

[12] Irenaeus, liber 5; Hippolytus *in oratione de consummatione mundi*; Theodoret in *Epitome divinorum decretorum*, capite de Antichristo; Suplpitius ex B. Martino, *libro 2, Dialogi*; Cyril *Catechesi* 15; Hillary, *in Matthaeum*, can. 25; Ambrose *in Lucam* lib 10, caput 21; Chrysostom, Augustine, and Cyril of Alexandria, in chapter 5 of John; Gregory *Moralium*, lib. 31; cap. 10; Damascene lib. 4, cap. 28.

although he could be from the tribe of Dan, will pretend that he is from the household of David. Next, all the Fathers very clearly teach that Antichrist will be a Jew, such as those twelve cited a little while ago, who say he is going to be from the tribe of Dan. Besides, Ambrose, *on 2 Thess. 2*, asserts that he will be circumcised; Jerome teaches in his commentary on Daniel 11 that he is going to be born from the Jewish people; St. Martin teaches that Antichrist is going to command that all be circumcised according to the law,[13] and St. Cyril asserts that he will be exceedingly zealous for the temple of Jerusalem to show himself to be from the progeny of David.[14] At length, even Gregory says that Antichrist is going to keep the Sabbath and all the other ceremonies of the Jews.[15]

From these we have the most evident proof that the Pope is not the Antichrist. For from the year 606, in which our adversaries say Antichrist came, it is certain that no Pope was a Jew, whether by race or religion or any other manner. It is also certain that the Pope to this point was never received by the Jews as a Messiah, but on the other hand is held as an enemy and a persecutor. For this reason they ask God in their daily prayers that God would give to the living Pope a good mind toward the Jews and that he might send a Messiah in their days who would liberate them from the power of the Pontiff, and a bishop such as the Supreme Pontiff especially is, which they call תנמון (tey-na-mon) but in Syriac means tail, and is opposed to head. For while we call a bishop the head of the people, they on the other hand call him a tail as an insult; the head is absent so that they might be prepared to receive a high

---

[13] Found in Sulpitius, *Dialog.*, lib. 2.

[14] *Catechesis* 15.

[15] Liber II, epist. 3.

priest as a head for their Messiah.

Therefore, R. Levi Gerson, in chapter 7 and 11 of Daniel, explains all those things which are said about Antichrist concerning the Roman Pontiff, whom he calls another Pharaoh and opposed to the coming Messiah. See the *orationes Mahasor*, fol. 26.

CHAPTER XIII
On the Seat of Antichrist

E continue to the sixth. Our adversaries impudently affirm that the particular seat of Antichrist is Rome, or even founded upon the apostolic throne at Rome. For they say Antichrist is going to invade the See of Peter, and will carry off the summit to the highest place and thence tyrannically preside over and dominate the whole Church. They try to show that Rome is the royal city of Antichrist from Apocalypse 17, where John, speaking on the seat of Antichrist, says it will be a great city which will sit upon seven hills and which has rule over the kings of the earth.

Moreover, they try to show that Antichrist will have his seat at Rome, not in the palace of Nero but in the very Church of Christ, from what Paul says in 2 Thess. 2, that Antichrist is going to sit in the temple of God. For when he says absolutely, "in the temple of God," they understand the true temple of the true God. There is no such thing unless it is the Church of Christ, since the temples of the Gentiles are true temples, but of demons, not God. Moreover, the temple of the Jews was indeed for God but had already ceased to be a temple when the sacrifice and priesthood of the Jews ceased. For these three (the temple, the sacrifice and the priesthood) are so joined that you cannot have one without the other. Besides, that temple of the Jews was laid desolate and never in the future to be rebuilt, as Daniel says: "And even to the end of the world the desolation will continue;"[1] therefore, the Apostle does not speak about it.

The argument is confirmed from the Fathers. Jerome says: "In the temple of God he will sit, either in Jerusalem as some men think, or in the Church, as we reckon is more true."[2] Oecumenius: "He did not say the temple of Jerusalem, but the Church of Christ."

Theodore Bibliander adds the testimony of Gregory, who wrote in a letter to John of Constantinople: "The king of pride is near, and it is not unlawful to say that an army of priests is prepared for him." From such words he takes up a two-fold argument. One is thus; John of Constantinople is said to be a precursor of Antichrist, because he wished to be called universal bishop; so that will be Antichrist, who really will make himself a universal bishop, and will sit in the Church as the head of all. On the other hand, the army of Antichrist will be priests therefore, Antichrist will be a prince of priests. From this the heretics reckon that they have clearly shown that the Roman Pontiff is Antichrist seeing that he rules at Rome, he sits in the temple of God and he is called Universal bishop as well as Prince of Priests.

Just the same, the true opinion is that the seat of Antichrist will be Jerusalem, not Rome, and the temple of Solomon as well as the throne of David, not the temple of St. Peter or the Apostolic See. We can prove the fact by a two-fold argument: First, by refutation, then from the Scriptures and the Fathers.

First, I will establish the argument. Let us say that Antichrist will sit in the Church of Christ and he will be held as prince and head of the Church, and in that he will

---

[1] Daniel 9:26-27.

[2] Quaest. 11 *ad Algasiam.*

manage magistracy and offices, as Melanchthon, Calvin and other heretics teach.[3] Moreover, the Roman Pope is Antichrist, as these writers teach in the same places; therefore, the Roman Pope sits in the true Church of Christ, and is the prince and head of the Church. But there can only be one true Church of Christ, just as Christ is one, as even Calvin teaches;[4] therefore, the Lutherans, Calvinists and all others are foreign to the Church, which is under the Pope, that is outside of the true Church of Christ.

Calvin sees this argument and responds that the Church is not under the Pope as much as the ruins of the Church of Christ are seen there. He says as much in the *Institutes*: "Still, as in ancient times, there remained among the Jews certain special privileges of a Church, so in the present day we do not deny that the Papists have those vestiges of a Church which the Lord has allowed to remain among them amid the dissipation. ... He provided by his providence that there should be other remains also to prevent the Church from utterly perishing. Yet, when they pull down buildings the foundations and ruins are often permitted to remain; so he did not suffer Antichrist either to subvert his Church from its foundation, or to level it to the ground, but was pleased that amid the devastation the edifice should remain, though half in ruins... Hence, we scarcely deny that churches remain under his tyranny."[5]

But, his solution provides two arguments for us. 1) If only the ruins of the Church of Christ remain, therefore, the Church of Christ is ruined; hence Truth lied when it

---

[3] Melancthon, *in apologia confes. Augustanae*, art. 6; Calvin, *Instit.*, lib. 4, cap. 2 § 12, and cap. 7 § 25; Illyricus, *Cent.* 1, lib. 2, cap. 4, col. 435.

[4] *Instit.*, lib. 4, cap. 1, § 2.

[5] Lib. 4, cap. 2, § 11-12.

said: "And the gates of hell will not prevail against it."[6] 2) The Church is ruined as well as its ruins and foundation, so that the Papists also hold semi-ruined buildings; therefore, the Lutherans and the Calvinists have no Church. For they do not have the whole Church of Christ, since it is now a ruin, and still the ruins remain; but they do not even have the edifice, for that is with the Papists under Antichrist. Therefore, what is it that they have? By chance a new building? But that which is new is not of Christ. But who, unless he were blind, does not see that he is safer in the true Church of Christ (even if an edifice), than to remain in nothing?

Now I come to the Scriptures whereby it is proved that the seat of the Antichrist is going to be in Jerusalem, not Rome. The first is in chapter 11 of the Apocalypse, where John says that Enoch and Elijah are going to fight with Antichrist in Jerusalem, and must be killed there by the same Antichrist: "And they will throw their bodies in the streets of the great city, which is spiritually called Sodom, and Egypt, where even their Lord was crucified." Arethas in this citation says: "Their bodies he will cast out unburied in the streets of Jerusalem, for in it he will reign as King of the Jews." Likewise, all other interpreters show, and this can rightly be said to be Jerusalem, and it cannot be denied. For what City is it in which the Lord was crucified but Jerusalem?

This is why Chytraeus, who would rather this city were Rome, passes over the words "Where even their Lord was crucified," as if they did not pertain to the matter, or as though he had not read them. Nor is it opposed to what Jerome says, when he tries to show that Jerusalem cannot be called Sodom, since everywhere in Scripture it is called the holy city. For in that epistle he persuades Marcellus

---

[6] Matthew 16:18.

that, after leaving Rome behind, he should come into Palestine and there he can heap up all those places in praise of Jerusalem and in censure of Rome, and try to excuse Jerusalem in every manner. Nor does he do it in his own name, but in the name of Paula and Eustochius, to whom he thought forgiveness must be given, if they were to explain something a little differently than the matter stood. That the earthly Jerusalem can be called Sodom on account of the lust and the crimes of the Jews is also clear from Isaiah, who when he prefaced a title to the first chapter: "The Vision of Isaiah, which he saw over Judah and Jerusalem," he next added: "Hear the word of the Lord, O princes of Sodom! Perceive with your ears the law of God, O my people Gomorrah!"

Further, it is not a valid argument that Jerusalem is called holy, therefore, it cannot be called Sodom. For just as in the same epistle Jerome says that Rome is called Babylon by John, and the purple whore on account of the heathen emperors, and still, the same is holy on account of the Church of Christ, and the tombs of Peter and Paul; so also Jerusalem is the holy city, on account of the prophets and apostles who preached there, on account of the cross of Christ and his tomb and like things yet still it is Sodom and Egypt on account of the crimes of infidelity of the Jews and their blindness.

The Second place is Apocalypse 17, where John says there will be ten kings who divide the Roman Empire, and from such rulers Antichrist will come, having hatred for the purple whore, that is Rome, and are going to lay waste to her and even burn her with fire. How, therefore, will it be the seat of Antichrist, if he should overturn and burn it at that time?

Add that, as we showed above, Antichrist will be Jewish, and the Messiah of the Jews, and a king; therefore, without a doubt he will constitute his seat in Jerusalem, and he will hasten to restore the temple of Solomon. For the Jews dream of nothing other than Jerusalem and the temple, nor do they seem ever to be going to receive anyone for a Messiah who would not sit in Jerusalem and restore the temple in some way. Lactantius says for this reason, that in the time of Antichrist the supreme kingdom is going to be in Asia and the West will serve, the East will rule.[7] He also determines the part of Asia in which this kingdom will be and says it will be Syria, that is, Judaea, which is part of Syria, and which is always called Syria by the Latins.[8] In like manner, Jerome and Theodoret, commenting on chapter XI of Daniel, gather from Daniel himself that Antichrist is going to set up his tents in the region of Jerusalem, and at length it will end on mount Olivet. Further, Irenaeus clearly said that Antichrist was going to rule in Jerusalem.[9]

The third place is in the words of Paul: "So that he would sit in the temple of God."[10] Although different expositions are given by the Fathers, some also understand through the temple of God the minds of the faithful, in which Antichrist is said to sit after he will have seduced them, as Anselm expresses. Some understand through the temple Antichrist himself, with his whole people; Antichrist would want himself and his own to seem the true spiritual temple of God, that is, the true Church, as Augustine explains.[11] There, he deduces this exposition from the manner of speaking which Paul uses, who did not

---

[7]   Lib. 7, cap. 15.

[8]   Ibid, cap. 17.

[9]   Lib. 5.

[10]   2 Thessalonians 2:4.

[11]   *De Civitate Dei*, lib. 20, cap. 19.

say in Greek ἐν τῷ ναῷ, (in the temple) but εἰς τὸν ναὸν, (into the temple), as if to say Antichrist will sit within the temple of God, that is, just as if he, with his own, were the temple of God. Although this annotation of Augustine is not necessary, for even if in Latin it is not correct when it says to sit within the temple, rather than in the temple, still in Greek it is not said incorrectly: καθέζουμαι εἰς τὴν ἐκκλησίαν, or εἰς τὸν ναὸν, as it is commonly read.

Some also understand the churches of Christians, which Antichrist will command to serve him, as Chrysostom interprets it. Still the exposition is the more common, probable and literal of those who teach that for the temple of God is understood the temple of Solomon, in whichever renewed temple that Antichrist will sit in. Especially in the New Testament, the churches of Christians are never understood for Temple of God; rather that is always understood as the temple in Jerusalem. What is more, the Latin and Greek Fathers for so many centuries never called the churches of Christians temples, which in Greek are called ναὸς, as St. Paul says in this passage; rather they call them εὐχτήρια, that is oratories, as churches, or houses of prayer, or basilicas, or martyria.

Certainly neither Justin Martyr, nor Irenaeus, nor Tertullian, nor Cyprian use the noun "temple" when they treat on the Churches of Christians, and Jerome says that Julian the Apostate ordered that the basilicas of the saints either be destroyed or turned into temples.[12]

Further, the reason why the Apostles do not call the churches of Christians temples is two-fold. 1) Because then they did not have any temples, but only certain places in private houses that they set aside for prayer, a sermon and the holy celebration of the Mass. 2) Because while the

---

[12] Ep. *Ad Riparium*.

memory of the Jewish temple still flourished, the Apostles were to introduce something similar to distinguish the church from the synagogue, so they avoided the use of the word "temple", just as on account of the same reckoning the Apostles in Scripture never call Christian priests "priests" [*sacerdotes*], but only bishops and elders. But after Jerusalem was destroyed and the temple burned, and the memory of the old temple and its priesthood abolished, everywhere the holy Doctors began to use the word "temple" and "priesthood".

Therefore, since the Apostle, writing that Antichrist was going to sit in the temple of God, said something which he wished to be understood by those to whom he wrote, and then they did not understand in the word "temple" anything else but the temple of Jerusalem, which appears for certain to be what the Apostle spoke about. But it is also confirmed from the common exposition of the Fathers.

Irenaeus says: "When Antichrist will have sat in the temple of Jerusalem, then the Lord will come."[13] Hippolytus the martyr (*loc. cit.*), says: "he will build a temple in Jerusalem." St. Martin (*loc. cit.*) teaches the same thing. Cyril of Jerusalem says: "What kind of temple does the Apostle speak of? In the temple that is the relic of the Jews. God forbid that it should happen in this, in which we are."[14] Hilary says on Matthew 25, "Antichrist, being received by the Jews, will stand in the place of sanctification." It is certain that he is talking about the temple of the Jews, for he calls it the place of sanctification, which is what Christ calls it in Matthew 24 when he said: "When you will have seen the abomination

---

[13]   Lib. 5.

[14]   *Catechesi* 15.

standing in the holy place." Ambrose says Antichrist, according to history, is going to sit in that temple in which the Romans threw in the head of a pig, in the time of the Emperor Titus; according to the mystical sense, he is going to sit in the interior temple of the Jews, that is, in their faithless minds.[15]

Sedulus explains, in this place of the Apostle, that in the temple of God, "He will try to restore the temple of Jerusalem, etc." John Damascene says: "In the temple, not ours, but the old Jewish temple."[16] Chrysostom, Theodoret, and Theophylactus (who say Antichrist is going to sit in the churches of Christians), also say he is going to sit in the temple of Solomon. Chrysostom says on this verse: "He will command himself to be worshiped as a God, and to be placed in the temple, not only in Jerusalem, but even in the churches." Theophylactus and Theodoret says the same thing; even Augustine and Jerome[17] do not deny Antichrist is going to sit in the temple of Solomon.

There is only Oecumenius, who denies that Antichrist is going to sit in the temple of the Jews, but he is the more recent of all of them, and by no means do we put him before the other Fathers. By chance his text might have been corrupted and lacked only one sentence, for it is strange that he would suddenly recede from Chrysostom, Theodoret and Theophylactus whom he otherwise always follows.

Now we respond to the arguments of our adversaries given above. To the first I respond in three ways. 1) It can

---

[15] In cap. 21 Lucae.

[16] lib. 4, cap. 28.

[17] Augustine, *De Civitate Dei*, lib. 20, cap. 19; Jerome, Quaest. 11 ad Algasiam.

be said with Augustine,[18] Aretha, Haymon, Bede and Rupert on chapter 17 of the Apocalypse, that for the whore which sits upon seven hills and has a kingdom over the kings of the earth, that Rome is not understood, but the universal city of the devil, which in scripture is always called Babylon and is opposed to the city of God, that is, the Church, which is called Jerusalem. Through the seven hills is understood the universality of the proud, and especially of the kings of the earth.

Secondly, it can be said, and in my judgment better, that for the whore is understood Rome, as Tertullian[19] and Jerome[20] explain it; but Rome ruling the heathen, worshiping idols and persecuting Christians, not Christian Rome, for the same authors explain it in the same way.

One must truly marvel at the impudence of the heretics, who, as they try and show the Roman Church to be the purple whore, use the testimony of Tertullian and Jerome. For in that time when, heathen Rome was contrary to Christian Rome, which, I ask, do those Fathers call the purple whore? If heathen Rome, why therefore do the heretics abuse the testimony? If Christian Rome, therefore, already then the Roman Church had already sunk and then Antichrist already reigned, which not even they concede. Besides, if Christian Rome was then Babylon, why does Tertullian say: "O happy church, into which the Apostles poured the whole doctrine with their own blood."[21] And why does Jerome, speaking about Rome, say: "I shall say to you, O great Rome you have blotted out the blasphemy written on your forehead by the confession of Christ"?

---

[18] In Ps. 26.

[19] Lib. *Contra Judaeos; contra Marcionem*, lib. 3.

[20] *Loc. Cit.*

[21] *Praescriptionibus contra haereticos.*

Next, the same is clear from John himself, who speaks about that Rome, which held empire over the kings of the earth and that was drunk in the blood of the saints and from the blood of the martyrs of Jesus. That certainly did not take place except in that Rome which cut down the martyrs under the rule of Nero and Domitian.

3) I say, although that woman could be Christian Rome, as the heretics would have it, still their argument has no force. As we showed above, Antichrist will have hatred towards Rome, in no matter what way he takes it up, and he will fight with it and lay it desolate, and burn it. From which it manifestly follows that Rome is not the seat of the Antichrist.

Now to the second argument: we have already said Paul treats on the temple of Solomon in that passage. Hence to the reasoning which we made, I respond: After the Jewish sacrifice and priesthood ceased that temple ceased to be a Jewish temple; but it did not immediately cease to be the temple of God. The same temple could have been the temple of Christians and really was so long as it remained. For the Apostles preached and gave praise there after the ascension of Christ and the arrival of the Holy Spirit, as is clear from the words of Luke: "They were always in the temple praising and blessing the Lord." We read the same in Acts 3: "Peter and John went up into the temple for the prayer at the ninth hour." And in Acts 5, the angel says to the Apostles: "Speak in the temple all the words of this life to the people."

To the argument from Daniel I respond: either Daniel would have it that the temple is not going to be rebuilt, except at the end of the world (which is true since Antichrist will be present at the end of the world); or it is going to remain desolate in eternity because although it will be rebuilt, still it will never be a temple not profaned after the destruction carried out by Titus. When it will be raised up by Antichrist, then the abomination of desolation will especially remain in it, i.e. either Antichrist himself or his image, or the temple will never be perfectly rebuilt, but will still be in the beginnings of rebuilding, and Antichrist is going to sit in that temple at its beginning stages.

We have already responded to the passages of the Fathers that either assert, or at least do not deny, that Antichrist is going to sit in the temple of Solomon. Many add the fact that Antichrist is also going to sit in the churches of Christians; that is true and not opposed to our position. The Fathers would not have it that Antichrist is going to sit in the Church as a bishop, like the heretics dream up, rather he is going to sit as a god. Antichrist will command all temples of the world to be converted to his worship, and he will make his own person worshiped. "He will command" (says Chrysostom on this citation), "himself to be worshiped as a God, and to be venerated and placed in the temple, not only in Jerusalem, but even in the churches." The rest speak in the same way.

Now to the arguments taken up from the words of St. Gregory the Great, I respond: from his words we deduce the contrary to those which the heretics have mustered. They argue thus: The bishop of Constantinople was a precursor of Antichrist, because he made himself universal bishop; therefore, Antichrist will be some universal bishop, who will usurp all things to himself. But the opposite is gathered, since a precursor ought not be the same with the one he foreshadows, but by far lesser, even if in some matter he is similar to him just as we see in John the Baptist and Christ. So if he is a precursor of Antichrist, who makes himself universal bishop, the true Antichrist himself will not make himself this, but something greater; without a doubt he will extol himself over everything that is called God. Or if the true Antichrist will only make himself a universal bishop, then John of Constantinople, who did this, was not a precursor of Antichrist, but the true Antichrist, which still Gregory never says, nor our adversaries. So the sense of the words of Gregory is that because Antichrist will be very proud, and the head of all the proud, so also he will suffer no equals; whoever usurps something not due to him and wishes to go beyond and be over others, he is a precursor to him. Such were the bishops of Constantinople, who, although in the beginning were only an archbishop, first usurped the title of patriarch, and then the title of universal.

With equal reasoning, when Gregory says: "an army of priests is prepared for him," he did not mean priests as in "priests pertain to the army of Antichrist", since he will gather his own in that army:; but priests as in the proud prepare an army for Antichrist, since he speaks on the same John and priests like him that elevated themselves unjustly above the rest. It does not follow that Antichrist will be a prince of priests, but prince of the proud.

From this chapter we have an outstanding argument that the Pope is not Antichrist, seeing that his seat is not in Jerusalem, nor in the temple of Solomon; nay more, it is believable that from the year 600 to the present (1589) no Roman Pontiff has been to Jerusalem.

CHAPTER XIV
On the Doctrine of Antichrist

N the doctrine of Antichrist there is a great deal of controversy between us and the heretics. It is certain from the Scriptures as well as from the testimony of our adversaries that there are going to be four points of doctrine of Antichrist.

1) He will deny that Jesus is the Christ and hence he will oppose all the things our Savior established, such as Baptism, Confirmation, etc. He will teach that circumcision and the Sabbath have not yet ceased, as well as other ceremonies of the old law. "Who is a liar, but he who denies that Jesus is the Christ? And this is Antichrist, who denies the Father and the Son, etc."[1]

2) After he will have persuaded the world that our Savior is not the true Christ, then he will assert that he is the true Christ promised in the law and Prophets. "If anyone will come in my name, you will receive him,"[2] that is as the Messiah.

3) He will declare that he is God and will demand to be worshiped as a god. "So that he shall sit in the temple, showing himself just as if he were God."[3]

4) He will not only say that he is God, but even that he alone is God and will oppress all other gods, i.e., both the true God and false gods, and all idols. "Who extols himself over everything which is called God, or that is

---

[1]   1 John 2:22.

[2]   John 5:43.

[3]   2 Thessalonians 2:4.

worshiped."[4] And in Daniel: "He will not think God is his
father, nor will he worship anything of the gods, because
he will rise against them all."[5]

All of these are true in some manner and pertain to
Antichrist; even our adversaries agree with us on this
point. But the question is on the understanding of these
four points. For Catholics understand simply according to
the words of Scripture that Antichrist is going to deny the
true Christ; he is going to make himself Christ; he is going
to preach that he is God; and he will curse all other Gods
and idols. From these four arguments we endeavor to show
the Pontiff is not Antichrist. It is certain the Pope does not
deny Jesus is Christ, nor has he introduced circumcision,
or the Sabbath in place of Baptism, and the day of the Lord.
In like manner, it is certain the Pontiff has not made
himself Christ or God, and it is especially certain, that not
only has he not made himself God (since he clearly
worships Christ and the Trinity), but our adversaries
maintain that he also worships idols and images and dead
saints.

Nevertheless, our adversaries by far read it otherwise.
They say in the first place that Antichrist is not openly
going to deny Jesus is the Christ by word, but by work,
because under the appearance of Christianity and the
Church he will corrupt the doctrine on the Sacraments, on
justification, etc. Calvin says: "We gather the tyranny of
Antichrist is such that he abolishes not the name of Christ
or the Church, but rather uses the name of Christ as a
pretext, and lurks under the name of Church as under a
mask."[6] The Centuriators of Magdeburg say: "Such is

---

[4]　Ibid.

[5]　Daniel 11:37.

[6]　*Instit.*, lib. 4, cap. 7, § 25.

certain, that while professing Christ in doctrine he will still
deny his office and merit... John shows that Antichrist is
going to deny that Christ came in the flesh, this is, that
Christ redeemed us wholly in his flesh and saved us; but
that good works will confer salvation upon us."[7] Next, they
say Antichrist is not going to make himself Christ or God
by his own word, but by work, because he will take up the
place of Christ and of God, making himself head of all the
faithful in the Church, which is proper to Christ alone. The
Centuriators remark: "He will show himself for God, that
he might be vicar of Christ and head of the Church, and
can set up and tear away the articles of faith."

Next, they say Antichrist is not going to reject idols;
nay more, he shall openly adore them and they try to show
from Daniel; after he had said Antichrist was going to rise
against all gods, he adds: "He will venerate the god
Moazim in his place, and a god whom their fathers did not
know, he will worship with gold and silver and precious
stones, etc."[8] For Moazim, however, the heretics
understand the Mass, images, relics and like things of
ornate temples. So Illyricus argues in his book *Contra
Primatum.*

Moreover, when the Apostle says that Antichrist is
going to elevate himself above everything which is called
God or which is worshiped, they try to prove this was
written about the Roman Pontiff, who makes himself vicar
of Christ and usurps greater authority than Christ had.
Illyricus tries to show it in his *Catalogue of Witnesses* (for
I have not seen how the rest try to show it), page 3.
Without a doubt, Christ declared nothing other than to
show himself to be God; nay more, to effect that he and his

---

[7] *Cent.* 1, lib. 2, cap. 4, col. 435.

[8] Daniel 11:38.

cult is above God, which is to come in the name of Christ; from which it follows that the Pope, who offers himself for Christ's vicar, is himself the truest Antichrist. Likewise, Christ subjected himself to Scripture, he did and suffered such things that he would fulfill the Scripture, while the Pope said that he can dispense against the Apostle and the Evangelist, to make straight crooked and vice versa. This is the chief point especially of the side of the doctrine of our adversaries on Antichrist which rests upon the Scripture alone through new glosses incorrectly explicated. It is a clear indication of the matter that they cannot even cite one interpreter or Doctor for their side.

Then let us begin from the first argument that Antichrist is going to openly deny Jesus is the Christ by public profession, and inasmuch as all his Sacraments will have been discovered he will trample them under foot. It is proved: 1) from the aforesaid, chapter 5 &6. For if Antichrist by nation and religion will be Jewish, and received by the Jews as a Messiah, as we have shown, certainly he will not preach our Christ, but will publicly oppose him. Otherwise, the Jews would receive our Christ through Antichrist, which is completely absurd. Besides, since there cannot be two Christs, how will Antichrist be able to thrust himself on the Jews as the Christ unless first he had taught that our Christ, who preceded him, was not really the true Christ?

2) It is proved from 1 John 2:22, "Who is a liar but he who would deny Jesus is the Christ? This is Antichrist." For all heretics who deny Jesus is the Christ are called Antichrists in some manner so, the true Antichrist himself will simply deny Jesus is the Christ in every way. It is confirmed because the devil is said to work the mystery of iniquity through heretics, because they deny Christ secretly, but the arrival of Antichrist is called revelation,

because he will openly deny Christ.

It is also proved by the Fathers. Hilary says the devil tried to persuade men through the Arians that Christ was not the natural son of God, but adopted; yet through Antichrist he is going to try to persuade men that he was not even adopted, so as to utterly extinguish the name of the true Christ.[9] Hippolytus the martyr says that the character of Antichrist will be that men are compelled to say: "I deny Baptism; I deny the sign of the Cross," and similar things. Augustine asks whether men are going to be baptized at all while Antichrist rages. At length, he answers: "Certainly they will be strong, both parents to baptize their children, and these who shall then first believe, that they shall conquer that strong one, even though he has been unbound."[10] Here St. Augustine presupposes that Antichrist is not going to permit them to be baptized, and still some pious parents would rather suffer than that their sons should be unbaptized.

Jerome says in his commentary on Daniel chapter XI: "Antichrist will rise from a modest nation; that is, from the people of the Jews, and he will be so lowly and despised that he will not be given royal honor, but he shall obtain rule both through treachery and deceit. He will do this because he will feign himself the leader of the covenant, that is the law, and the covenant of God." There, Jerome teaches that Antichrist is going to acquire rule over the Jews, because he will show himself zealous for the Judaic laws. Sedulius, commenting on 2 Thessalonians 2:6, says that Antichrist is going to restore all Jewish ceremonies so as to abolish the gospel of Christ. Gregory says: "Because Antichrist will compel the people to judaize so that he

---

[9] *De Trinitate*, lib. 6.

[10] *De Civitate Dei*, lib. 20, cap. 8.

might restore the rite of the exterior law, he will want the Sabbath to be kept to place the faithlessness of the Jews in himself."

Then, in the time of Antichrist, all public offices and divine sacrifices will cease on account of the vehemence of the persecution, as we showed above in chapter III. It is evident from this that Antichrist is not going to corrupt the doctrine of Christ under the name of a Christian, as the heretics would have it. Rather, he will openly assault the name of Christ and the Sacraments while introducing Jewish ceremonies. Since the Pope does not do that, it is evident that he is not Antichrist.

Moreover, Antichrist will say openly that he is the Christ by name, not his minister, or vicar, as is clear especially from the very words of the Lord: "If another will come in my name, you will receive him."[11] There, the Lord seems to add on purpose "*in his own name,*" foreseeing that the Lutherans and Calvinists were going to say that Antichrist was not coming in his name, but in the name of our Christ as if he were his vicar.

Besides, the Fathers everywhere teach this. Irenaeus said: "He will try to show that he is Christ." Ambrose says: "He will argue from the Scriptures that he is Christ."[12] Theodoret says: "He will declare that he is Christ."[13] St. Cyril of Jerusalem said: "He will induce a certain man to falsely call himself the Christ, and through this title of Christ he will deceive the Jews who await him."[14] All the Fathers, as we showed above, say Antichrist will be received briefly as a Messiah by the Jews; thus he will

---

[11] John 5:43.

[12] *In Caput* 21 *Lucae.*

[13] In 2 Thess. 2.

[14] *Catechesi,* 15.

openly and by name make himself the Messiah, that is, the Christ. Hence the Roman Pontiff, who does not do this, as is known, is not Antichrist. For this very reason that he calls himself the vicar of Christ, he asserts that he is not Christ, but his minister.

The fact that Antichrist will openly declare himself to be God and desire to be worshiped as God, not only by usurping some authority of God, but by the name of God itself, is proved from the express words of the Apostle in 2 Thessalonians 2: "So that he will sit in the temple of God, revealing himself as though he were God." Paul not only says that Antichrist is going to sit in the temple (for even we sit in temples yet still we are not Antichrists), but he even explains the manner in which he will sit, that he will sit as a god, the only one to whom the temple is properly raised. In Greek this is much more clear. For he does not say: ὡς θεὸς, as a god, but ὁτι ἐστιν θεὸς; that is, revealing that he is God. All the Fathers so understand that verse.

Irenaeus says: "Proving to be an apostate and a robber, he will wish to be worshiped as if he were God." Chrysostom said on that verse: "He will command that he be worshiped for God, and be placed in the temple." He says elsewhere on this same verse: "He will confess himself as God of all."[15] Ambrose, commenting on 2 Thessalonians 2, said: "He will assert that he is God himself, not the Son of God." They all explain the verse similarly. From that we understand that the Roman Pontiff, who does not claim to be God, but the servant of God, is not Antichrist.

Furthermore, Antichrist is not going to permit any god, whether true, false or an idol, and this is proved from the very words of Paul in the same passage: "Who is extolled above everything which is called God, or that is worshiped." Here, we must remark that for "that which is

---

[15] *Homil.* 40.

worshiped," the Greek is σέβασμα which the Centuriators think means worship, that is, *the act of worshiping*, not *that which is worshiped*. From there, they try to show that the Apostle would have it that Antichrist is not going to adore idols, but is going to distort the worship of the true God by mutilating the Sacraments or by adding various ceremonies. Yet, certainly σέβασμα properly means not the act but the object, that is what is worshiped, such as an altar, shrines, idols, etc. Worship is σέβας, or θεοσέβεια, not σέβασμα. This is why the Paul himself says in Acts 17: "Διερχόμενος γὰρ καὶ ἀναθεωρῶν τὰ σεβάσματα ὑμῶν ἑυρον καὶ βωμὸν, etc." He says "Disregarding and considering your idols, I discover the altar, etc." Here Paul clearly means through σεβάσματα the very things that are worshiped, such as the shrines, altars and idols. We also read in Wisdom: Κρεῖττον γὰρ ἐστὶν τῶν σεβάσματων αὐτοῦ ων αὐτὸς μὲν ἔζησεν ἐκεῖνα δὲ οὐδέποτε. That is: "Man is better than the idols (σεβάσματων) which he made. For he lives for a time, but they do not."[16] I do not know from what source someone would so dare to twist things to deny that σεβασμάτων means idols themselves, or simulacra, which men make with their hands: things that seem to have life when they do not live.

Therefore, all Greek texts (even that of Erasmus, whom all the heretics celebrate, both in his version and in annotations), teach that σέβασμα ought to be rendered as a god. Next, the words of Daniel are rather clear: "He will not worship any of the gods, but will rise against them all." Jerome, writing on that verse, says this cannot be understood to mean Antiochus, as Porphyrius thought, because it is certain Antiochus worshiped the Greek gods; but it can be understood on Antichrist who will worship no

---

[16]   Wisdom 15:17.

god.

At last we come to the consensus of the Fathers. Irenaeus said: "Indeed he will put away the idols and will lift himself up as the one idol."[17] Hippolytus from the same sermon on the end of the world says: "Antichrist will not permit idolatry." Cyril of Jerusalem says: "Antichrist will hate idols."[18] St. John Chrysostom says on this place in Daniel: "He is extolled above everything which is called God, or divinity. For he will not induce to idolatry." Theophylactus, Oecumenius, and Theodoret all teach the same thing, and the last beautifully notes that the devil wondrously fools and is going to fool the sons of perdition. For of old he persuaded that there were many gods and that various idols must be worshiped, and in that way he took a great profit. In the time of Antichrist, however, because he will see that through the doctrine of Christ idols and the multitude of false gods have been expunged through nearly the whole world, he also will accuse idols and their multitude and in that way will still deceive men. In this it seems the Pope, who according to Catholics acknowledges God the Father and the Son and the Holy Spirit, and according to the heretics worships many idols, in no way can be called the Antichrist.

But they say Daniel chapter 11 affirms that the God Moazim must be worshiped with gold, silver and precious stones.

The first response is that though the god Moazim, which is interpreted as strength (that is, very strong), Antichrist himself can be understood. Accordingly, that "He will be venerated," in Hebrew is not יִשְׁתַּחֲוֶה (yah-shea-ti-ka-veh), he will worship, but יְכַבֵּד (ya-ka-bed), he

---

[17] Loc. Cit.

[18] *Catech.*, 15.

will glorify. In the same way, in Psalm 90 (91) God says: "I will raise him and glorify him." In Hebrew that is אסבללדהו (eh-ka-bey-day-hu), and certainly God is not going to glorify men by subjecting them to themselves but by exalting them. Therefore, Antichrist will glorify himself when he will be worshiped by all. For this reason the Septuagint renders this δοξάσει, and Theodoret expresses it in this way: "For this 'Moazim' means a strong and powerful god, and he will call himself this. For he placed it in his own place for himself. He will raise temples to himself, and adorn them with gold, silver, precious stones."

The second response, which I prefer, is that Antichrist is going to be a magician and by the custom of other magicians he will worship the devil secretly, by whose work he will do wonders. He will call this one whom he is going to adore Moazim. Hence, for Moazim we do not think the name of a god, but of a certain strong and secret place in which the special treasures of Antichrist will be and where he will worship the devil himself. For it follows from Daniel that he will also see to it that he fortifies Moazim with a strong god whom he knows. And truly מעוז (ma-koz) means both a strong place and a citadel, as Nicholas Lyranus explains it. Moreover, it must necessarily be said that Antichrist is himself the god Moazim, or if he is someone else, Antichrist must worship him only in a very secret place, secret from all others. The very words of Daniel compel us that otherwise they would oppose themselves; if he will worship no god, how will he openly worship an idol?

Now, the two arguments of Illyricus are very weak. In the first argument he errs three times. First, he asserts that the words of Paul were explained by Christ, when it ought to be the other way around. Secondly, he errs in saying say in Matthew 24 that to come in the name of Christ means the same thing as to be the Vicar of Christ. For the very explanation of Christ is opposed to this argument of Illyricus. When the Lord says: "Many will come in my name," soon he adds: "saying, I am Christ." There, to come in the name of Christ is to usurp the name of Christ to one's own person. Once, Simon Magus did this very thing, as Irenaeus witnessed,[19] and in our times David Georgius. At length, Antichrist will do this very thing. But the Pope, because he calls himself the Vicar of Christ, does not make himself Christ.

Thirdly, Illyricus errs because he makes Christ an inept interpreter of Paul. For he does not rightly explain what Paul said: "Extol himself over every thing that is God" for the verse: "many will come in my name," that is, as he sees it, make themselves my vicar. The vicar of God is not over everything that is God, but below it, just as the vicar of a king is below everything of the king. It cannot be thought or pretended that one who professes himself to be the vicar of some king will boast to be above all kings. From that we see the blindness and impudence of our adversaries who babble this nonsense which they would abhor in its common meaning.

Now, I respond to the argument of Illyricus, where he argued that the Pope usurped a greater authority than even Christ had. The proposition and assumption of this argument involves two lies, and besides the consequence avails to nothing. 1) It is false that Christ subjected himself to the Scriptures since it should be certain that he is the author of the Scriptures, and hence above them. Moreover, when we read Christ did what he did so as to fulfill the Scriptures, the *that* is not a cause but means the event, as Chrysostom and Augustine teach in chapter 12 of John. Christ did not die because Isaiah wrote this, but Isaiah

---

[19]   Lib. 1, cap. 20.

wrote this because it was going to happen.

Next, it is also false that the Pope ever said by word or deed that he can dispense against the Evangelists or Apostles. For even if he can dispense on some precept placed by the Apostles, still this is not against the Apostle but according to him, who without a doubt knew the Apostolic power whereby he, being put in charge of something, stood in the Church for a time; and that there were going to be successors, that they could moderate or change the same things so long as it would be expedient for the Church. But no Catholic ever said a Pontiff can dispense in any way from the Gospel, i.e., the divine precepts.

Then the consequent is bad. In the major proposition Illyricus speaks on the subjection of Christ to the Scriptures, not in regard to precept, but to prophecies, while Illyricus is not ignorant that Christ abolished the Sabbath and abrogated the ceremonial law. Yet in the minor he speaks about precepts, and so the argument has four ends, and thence nothing can be concluded.

This will be sufficient in this place on the doctrine of Antichrist.

CHAPTER XV
On the Miracles of Antichrist

HOLY SCRIPTURE contains three things about the miracles of Antichrist. 1) He is going to do many miracles. 2) These will be of some quality. 3) Three examples are posited. The Apostle teaches in 2 Thessalonians 2 that Antichrist is going to do miracles, saying: "His arrival will be accompanied by signs and wonders according to the operation of Satan." The Lord says in the Gospel of Matthew: "They will give signs and great wonders, so that, if it is possible, even the elect will be led into error." He said, "They will give," not "he will give." This is because not only Antichrist, but his ministers, will perform signs, to the extent that St. Gregory said even the torturers of the holy martyrs are going to perform signs and wonders at that time.[1] Next, in Apocalypse 13, "And he will perform great signs in the sight of men." Paul explains what type they will be in Thessalonians, saying in one word, they will be lies: "In all power, signs and lying portents."

Hence the signs will be lies by an account of all the causes, final, efficient, material and formal. For the end of those miracles will be to show Antichrist is God and the Messiah, which will be the most pernicious lie. Chrysostom teaches in this place, that these lies are called miracles because they will induce men to lie. And Ambrose in this place teaches that the purpose of the miracles of Antichrist are going to be that he will try to show himself to be God,

---

[1] *Moral.*, lib. 32, cap. 12.

just as our Christ proved his divinity with true miracles.

Next, the signs are called lies in regard to their efficient cause; for the principal efficient cause will be the father of lies, that is the devil. For the Apostle speaks thus: "His arrival according to the operation of Satan." And all the Fathers assert Antichrist is going to be an outstanding magician. Moreover, the devil is going to dwell in him in his very conception, or at least from infancy, and through him perpetrate signs.

St. Cyril of Jerusalem also teaches that Antichrist is going to be a magician, and instructed in sorcery, incantations and evil arts, he shall announce himself; his miracles are called lies because they begin from the father of lies.[2]

There will also be many lies from those by reason of the material cause, because there will be certain imaginary deceptions, as Cyril says above and Theodoret teaching on the same places of Scripture. For he will appear to raise the dead and heal the sick, but they will be illusions of demons, not true miracles. Due to the fact that in Apocalypse 13 Antichrist is said to be going to do miracles in the sight of men, i.e., appearances and delusions in the sight of men, not solid and true as Arethas remarks in the same place.

Next, there will be certain lies from those miracles by reckoning of the form, although they will be true from a reckoning of the matter, because it will seem that true things will be worked, but they will not conquer the power of the whole nature. Therefore, they will not formally be true miracles. True miracles are only called those which can be done by God, that is, which do not have natural causes, nor secret or manifest ones. Therefore, these miracles are not only in the sight of men, but even in the sight of demons and angels. But the miracles of Antichrist

2 *Catechesis* 15.

will all have natural causes, though they be secret from men.

In the Apocalypse,[3] they place three examples of the miracles of Antichrist. One, that he will cause fire to come down from heaven. The second, that he will make an image of the beast speak. Third, that he will feign himself to be dead and resurrect. Due to these particular miracles nearly the whole world will admire him.

From such miracles there will be two true earlier ones (true in regard to matter, not form), but the third will be no miracle at all.

Moreover, it could be objected against this that they do not all seem to be miracles attributed to Antichrist. For John, in that place, introduces two beasts, one which has seven heads, one of which seems to be dead and rises again. The second smaller one makes fire descend from heaven and the image speak. Therefore, if Antichrist will be before the beasts, these two miracles of the fire and image are not attributed to him; if he will be later than the beast, then the miracle of the resurrection cannot be attributed to him.

I respond: the first beast means either the Roman Empire or the multitude of the impious, as we said above, while one that is the head which seems to be dead and resurrects, is Antichrist. He will also be the supreme and last head of the impious; he will be the last king who will hold the Roman Empire, still without the name of Roman Emperor. And the Fathers teach that this feigned miracle of the resurrection is also certainly to be attributed to Antichrist.[4] St. Gregory argued in an epistle against Lyranus, who thought it was about the son of a certain

---

[3]   Apocalypse 13:14-15.

[4]   Primasius, Bede, Haymo, Richardus, Rupertus and Anselm interpreting Apocalypse 13.

Cusro, the King of Persia, whom he pretended was wounded in a battle but still not killed.[5] For no other proven history relates such a tale about the son of Cusro, nor can what follows in the Apocalypse agree with the son of Cusro: "And the whole world will admire the beast, saying who is like the beast?"

Hence, the second beast in the Apocalypse, according to Rupert, means the same Antichrist. The same Antichrist is expressed through two beasts: The first by reason of royal power and tyranny, whereby he will violently compel men; the other by reason of magical arts whereby he will subtly seduce men. Still, according to Richardus, Anselm and others, the second beast means the preachers of Antichrist, who will try to show with miracles that Antichrist is the true Messiah. Therefore, all these miracles will be either of Antichrist, or of his ministers. Thus, it follows that the Pope is not Antichrist, seeing that no Pontiff has ever feigned that he was dead and risen again, nor has he or any of his ministers ever made fire come down from heaven or an image speak.

But the Centuriators object that the Pope has made many lying miracles: "Such as visions of souls talking from purgatory, and asking Masses to be said for them and the healing of plagues, such as happened to those worshiping statues or calling upon the saints."[6]

I respond: In the first place, these are not the miracles which John writes that Antichrist is going to do; he will die and rise, make fire fall from heaven and to give the power of speech to an image. Therefore, let them show any Pope who did these signs, let alone any bishop. Next, these three kinds of things that they say are the miracles of Antichrist

---

[5]   Lib. XI, epist. 3.

[6]   *Cent.* 1, lib. 2, cap. 4, co. 436.

were used in the Church before that time in which our adversaries said Antichrist came openly. St. Gregory writes about Paschasius the Deacon, who lived in the time of Pope Symmachus, around the year 500.[7] His soul appeared to St. Germain, the bishop of Capu,a asking the bishop to pray for him so that he might be freed from the torments of purgatory. Certainly, this miracle happened a hundred years before "Antichrist appeared," in the opinion of all the heretics of this time. For no man places the arrival of Antichrist until after the year 600 and around the death of Gregory I. The same Gregory relates other apparitions of souls, asking for Masses.[8]

On the miracles of healing from the veneration of images, Eusebius relates an example of a bronze statue made of the Savior in the spot where the Lord cured a woman from the flow of blood. A certain plant customarily grew under that statue which rose even to the fringes of the image, and it cured anyone who touched it of all types of evils.[9] It is evident from such a miracle that God wished to approve the cult of holy images.

On the healing divinely conceded to those who had vowed something to the saints, there are innumerable testimonies among the Fathers and an outstanding testimony is extant in Theodoret. He writes that in his own time the temples of the martyrs were full of pictures or simulacra of hands, feet, eyes, heads and other human members, whereby various gifts of healing were shown, which men received from the holy martyrs for a matter of devotion.[10]

---

[7] *Dialog.* Lib. 4, cap. 40.

[8] Ibid, lib. 4, cap. 55.

[9] *Hist. Eccl.*, lib. 7, cap. 14.

[10] Theodoret, lib. 8 *ad Graecos*, which is on the martyrs.

CHAPTER XVI
On the Kingdom and Battles of Antichrist

E READ four things in the Scriptures about the kingdom and battles of Antichrist. 1) Antichrist shall come forth from the lowest place and will receive the rule over the Jews by frauds and treachery. 2) He is going to fight with three kings, namely over Egypt, Libya and Ethiopia, and at length will occupy their kingdoms. 3) He is going to add to himself seven other kings, and in that way evade the monarchy of the whole world. 4) With a countless army he will persecute Christians throughout the world, and this is the battle of Gog and Magog. It manifestly follows that none of these things agree with the Roman Pontiff, so that he in no way can be called Antichrist.

Daniel speaks on the first point: "He will stand, despised in his place, and neither honor nor royalty will be given him, and he will come secretly and obtain a kingdom in deceit."[1] St. Jerome writes in this place that these are also understood as concerning Antiochus Epiphanies; still by far they are more perfectly fulfilled in Antichrist. In just the same way, the things which are said in Psalm 71 (72) about Solomon are understood on Solomon himself, but are more perfectly fulfilled in Christ. For that reason the same Jerome, after he had shown this place on Antiochus, having followed Porphryius, so added: "We, however, interpret better and more rightly that in the end of the world Antichrist is going to do this, who has his rise from

---

[1]   Daniel 11:21.

a small nation, that is, the people of the Jews, and will be so lowly and despised that royal honor would not be given him, and through plotting and deceit he shall obtain rule, etc." Jerome means, this is the common exposition of Christians. Daniel in chapter 7 also compares Antichrist with a small horn because of its worthless and obscure beginning.

Yet this definitely does not agree with the Roman Pontiff in any manner, or it would be necessary for one to say that the Roman Pontiff, even to the year 600, was very obscure and of no name, and then quickly through deceit began to occupy some high place, but this is certainly false. For as Augustine says: "In the Roman Church the rule of the Apostolic See always flourishes."[2] Prosper of Aquitaine said: "Rome is made greater through the rule of priesthood in the citadel of religion, than in the throne of power."[3] And the Council of Chalcedon, in an epistle to Leo, asserted that at Rome the apostolic rays shine so that from there they expand to all and communicate their goods with everyone else. Next, even the heathen writer Ammianus Marcellinus, writing on the schism of Damasus and Ursicinus, says that he did not marvel if men contend with such zeal for the Roman Pontificate, since it has such power and importance.

Daniel speaks on the second point in chapter 7: "I considered the horns and behold, that small horn arose from the midst of the others, and tore out three from the first horns from his face. ... Hence the ten horns will be ten kings and another will rise after them. He will be more powerful than the first, and he will lay the three kings low." And explaining who these three kings are in chapter

---

[2] Epistle 162.

[3] *De vocatione Gentium*, liber 2, cap. 6.

11: "He will send his hand into the earth and the land of Egypt will not put him to flight, and he will be in control of the treasures of gold, silver and all the precious things of Egypt. He will also pass through Lybia and Ethiopia." St. Jerome, writing on these citations, and especially chapter 7, says: "Let us say what all Ecclesiastical writers hand down, that at the end of the world, when the kingdom of the Romans was to be destroyed, there were going to be ten kings who divide the Roman world amongst themselves, and an eleventh little king (Antichrist) was going to rise up who was going to conquer three of the ten kings, that is Egypt, Africa and Ethiopia; after they are dead, the other seven kings will submit their necks to the victor." Other Fathers writing on Daniel 7 and 11 teach the same thing on the three kings killed by Antichrist.[4]

This especially refutes the insanity of the heretics who argue the Pope is Antichrist. Let them say, if they can, at what time the Roman Pontiff slew the kings of Egypt, Lybia and Ethiopia, and occupied their kingdom? Theodore Bibliander, in his *Chronicle*, says that the Roman Pontiff is just as a little horn that first tore off one of the horns from the beast when Gregory II excommunicated the Greek Emperor Leo the Iconoclast, and forbade taxes to be rendered to him from Italy, and little by little occupied his territory, that is, he obtained the Exarchate of Ravenna. Second, he says the horn tore off another when Pope Zachary deposed Childeric, the king of the Franks, and commanded Pepin to be made king in his place. He does not say the third clearly, but seems to indicate that the third horn was torn off when Gregory VII excommunicated and deposed the Emperor Henry IV. There is a certain epistle extant from Emperor Frederick II, written against

---

[4] Irenaeus, lib. 5; Lactantius, lib. 7, cap. 16; Theodoret in cap. 7 et 11 Danielis.

the Pope, in which he asserted three horns had been torn
out by Antichrist, the kingdoms of Italy, Germany and
Sicily, which the Roman Pontiff especially compelled to
serve him.

But these are most untrustworthy. For in the first place,
Daniel does not speak about France or Germany, but
Egypt, Libya and Ethiopia. Next, no Pope has ever killed
their kings, but Antichrist will kill three kings, as St.
Jerome says. Besides, Antichrist will take possession of
their kingdoms, not hand them over to others. Yet the Pope
did not take the kingdom of France for himself, but gave it
to Pepin and after deposing the Emperor, bid another to be
created; so he did not usurp the empire to himself. In like
manner, when the Pope deprived Emperor Leo of the rule
of Ravenna he did not take possession of it himself, but
permitted it to the kings of the Lombards. Pepin, after the
Lombards were conquered, gave it to the Pope. Next, if to
depose princes is to tear out the horns, there will not be
three, but many more torn out by Antichrist. For it is
certain that apart from Leo III, Childeric and Henry IV, the
Popes have deposed many others: Innocent III deposed
Otho IV; Innocent IV deposed Frederick II. All six of these
lost their empire.

On the third, we have the clear testimony of the
Fathers. Lactantius and Irenaeus say that after three of the
ten kings will be killed by Antichrist, the other seven will
be subjected and he will be the ruler of them all.[5] Jerome
remarking on chapter 9 of Daniel where it says, "And he
will do what his fathers did not," says: "None of the Jews
except for Antichrist will ever have ruled the whole
world." Chrysostom asserts in his commentary on 2
Thessalonians 2 that Antichrist was going to be a monarch
and succeed the Romans in Monarchy, just as the Romans

---

[5]   Lactantius, lib. 7, cap. 16; Irenaeus, lib. 5.

succeeded the Greeks, the Greeks the Persians, and the Persians the Assyrians.

Next, St. Cyril of Jerusalem says that Antichrist is going to obtain the monarchy which beforehand was of the Romans.[6] This is sufficiently deduced from the opinion of the Fathers and Apocalypse, chapter 17, where we read: "And ten horns, which you saw, are ten kings. These have one plan, and power, and they will hand their rule to the beast." That this in no way agrees with the Roman Pontiff is certain. For the Pope was never a king over the whole world.

On the fourth, John says in the Apocalypse, chapter 20: "And the thousand years were ended; Satan was freed from his prison and went out, and seduced the nations, which are over the four corners of the earth with Gog and Magog, and he will gather them into battle, the number of which is like the sand of the sea. And they went up over the breadth of the earth, and surrounded the camp of the saints and the chosen city. And fire came down from heaven and devoured them, and the devil, who seduced them, was sent into the lake of fire and sulphur, where both the beast and the false prophets were tortured day and night for ever and ever." In these words the last persecution and its end are described. St. Augustine says the following about this: "This will be the last persecution before the impending judgment, which the holy Church will suffer throughout the world, the whole city of Christ by the whole city of the devil, in whatever degree each will be over the earth."[7] Similar things are in Ezechiel 38 and 39, which must be briefly explained on account of the many errors that arise from it.

---

6 *Catechisis* 15.

7 *De Civitate Dei*, lib. 20, cap. 11.

CHAPTER XVII
On Gog and Magog

HEREFORE, the first opinion, or rather error, is of the Jews, who teach that Gog is Antichrist, and Magog is the innumerable Scythian nations that hide within the Caspian mountains. Gog is going to come, that is Antichrist, with Magog, that is, with this army of Scythians, in the time which the Messiah will appear in Jerusalem; and then battle will be joined in Palestine, and there is going to be such a slaughter in the army of God, that for seven years the Jews will have no need to cut wood from trees to build fires because they will have spears, shields and like instruments thrown down everywhere with dead bodies, and then the golden age will come.

Jerome relates this opinion while commenting on chapter 38 of Ezechiel, as well as the writings of Peter the Galatian,[1] and Rabbi David Khimhi in their commentaries on the Psalms. Firstly, what they think is the coming battle of Gog and Magog that will take place is the first coming of Christ, confounding the first with the second, since the Scriptures clearly teach in the first coming Christ is going to come with humility, and finally will be immolated just as a tame sheep.[2] Secondly, that they think Antichrist is going to come to fight against them and with their Messiah is erroneous, since Antichrist really is going to be their Messiah, and will fight against the true Christ, our Savior,

---

[1] *Contra Judaeos*, lib. 5, cap. 12.

[2] Isaiah 53.

on behalf of the Jews.

The second opinion is of Lactantius, who thinks the battle of Gog and Magog is going to be a thousand years after the death of Antichrist.[3] He teaches that Antichrist is coming six thousand years from the beginning of the world and will reign for three and a half years. Then Antichrist must be killed; Christ will appear and the resurrection is going to happen, and the saints will rule with Christ there for a thousand years in the greatest peace and tranquility; meanwhile the infidels will not be exterminated, but will serve them peacefully. Again, after a thousand years the devil will be loosed again, and a most atrocious war will be aroused in all nations, where those who served the saints for a thousand years will fight against the same saints, and this is the battle of Gog and Magog, about which Ezechiel and John speak. But a little while later, all the impious will be slaughtered and then the second resurrection is going to take place, and the world will be completely renewed.

This opinion was also of many of the older Fathers, such as Papias, Justin Martyr, Irenaeus, Tertullian, Apollinaris and of a few others, as Jerome relates in chapter 36 of Ezechiel, and Eusebius.[4] But for a long time it had been refuted as an investigated error. For the Lord clearly teaches that after the persecution of Antichrist the last judgment will immediately follow.[5] Then, all the good are going to eternal life, while all the wicked into the eternal fire, hence there is not going to be another thousand years, nor any battle.[6]

---

[3] Lib. 7, cap. 24-26.

[4] *Hist.*, lib. 3, last chapter.

[5] Matthew 24:9-14.

[6] Translator's note: This opinion, common in some of the early Fathers, is called Chilism, or Millenarianism, and today, under a different form, the "Rapture." The early Fathers treat it as an opinion,

The third opinion is of Eusebius. He thought that Gog is the Roman emperor, and Magog his empire. But this rests upon a false foundation, for he deduces this opinion from chapter 24 of Numbers, where according to the Septuagint we read: "The kingdom of Gog will be lifted up, and his kingdom increased. God led him from Egypt, etc." There the Scripture seems to say that when Christ will return from Egypt in his time of infancy, then the kingdom of God will be lifted up. But it is certain that while Christ was an infant no kingdom was lifted up except that of the Romans.

But without a doubt this has been corrupted in this edition of the Septuagint. For the Hebrew does not have Gog, but Agag וידרמ מאגג מלכי (vey-ya-dom me-agag ma-ley-ko), "and it will be abolished on account of Agag," or his king before Agag. And the sense is, according to Jerome, commenting chapter 38 of Ezechiel, that the first King of Israel, Saul, was removed on account of Agag because he will sin by not killing him. Or according to others, Saul will be raised up before Agag, that is he will prevail and conquer Agag himself. Both are true, and that citation of Numbers is certainly understood to be about the kingdom of the Jews, not about Christ or the Romans. For it begins: "How beautiful are thy tabernacles, O Jacob, thy tents, O Israel, etc."

The fourth opinion is of others, who understand the wars of the devil through Gog and Magog and his angel, formerly completed in heaven with the good angels. Jerome refutes this, just as he refutes the literal argument in chapter 38 of Ezechiel.

The fifth is of Theodore Bibliander whom Chytraeus follows in his commentary on Apocalypse 20. Therefore,

---

and the later Fathers universally reject it, as do all later theologians. It appears to originate first in the early Father Papias.

Bibliander in his *Chronology*, accurately treats on Gog and
Magog, and at length teaches that the prophecies of
Ezechiel and John do not pertain to the same time. Instead,
the prophecy of Ezechiel was fulfilled in the time of the
Maccabees, whereas Gog and Magog were Alexander the
Great and his posterity that were kings of Syria and Egypt
that enjoined battles with the Jews and at length were
conquered by the Maccabees. But the prophecy of John
was fulfilled in the time of Pope Gregory VII and as many
pontiffs who followed him, thus Gog and Magog were
Popes, and other Christian princes and their armies, who
so long fought against the Saracens for the holy land, and
to recuperate the tomb of the Lord.[7] The first part of this
opinion is also that of Theodoret in his commentary on
Ezechiel 38, but it cannot be defended. Firstly, because
without a doubt the prophecies of Ezechiel and John are
one and the same, and hence each must be fulfilled after
the coming of Christ. For John says the army of Gog is
going to come from the four corners of the earth; Ezechiel
says the same thing, namely showing the army of Gog is
going to be Persians from the East, Ethiopians from the
South, Tubal, that is, Spanish from the West, and Togorma,
that is, Phrygians from the northern parts. Next John says
that this army must perish from fire sent from heaven, and
Ezechiel asserts the same thing at the end of chapter 36.
"Fire and sulphur will rain above him and over his army."
Next, John adds to this battle the renewal of Jerusalem,
that is, the glorification of the Church and in a similar vein
Ezechiel from chapter 40 even to the end of the book treats
on nothing but the wonderful renewal of Jerusalem.

Besides it is proved in the second place that the
prophecy of Ezechiel was not fulfilled in the time of the
Maccabees. In Ezechiel 38, it is said to Gog "you will come

---

[7] *Chronologia*, tab. 14.

at the end of your years." But Alexander the Great came in the middle of his years. Next, Ezechiel says that in the army of Gog there are going to be Ethiopians, Libyans, Spanish, Cappadocians, etc, who still never fought against Jerusalem, and particularly not in the time of the Maccabees. For the Syrians and Egyptians alone fought against them.

Next, Ezechiel describes such a victory against Gog and Magog, that afterwards there would be no fear of enemies; rather it was going to be the end of all battles. But such was not the victory of the Maccabees against the kings of Syria and Egypt. For the Jews never completely conquered the kingdom of Syria or Egypt, and a little after the Jews were again disturbed by the Romans, captured and never freed from their hands, as Augustine deduced from the history.[8] Therefore, the prophecy of Ezechiel was not fulfilled before the times of Christ.

The second part of the opinion of Bibliander, which is his own, is not only false but impious. For in the first place John speaks of the battle of Gog and Magog that is going to be against the camp of the saints, and the chosen city, that is, against the true Church of God. But the war of Christians to recover the Holy Land was wholly against Muslims, unless by chance Bibliander would have it that the Muslims are the true Church of God and the camp of the saints. Next, John says that men are going to be in the army of God from the four corners of the earth, but in the Christian army they were only from the West and the North, that is French, Germans and Italians. Besides, John says that after the war of Gog and Magog Jerusalem would be renewed and glorified; the devil, Antichrist and the false prophets are going to be cast out into the eternal fire. On the other hand, the war of the Christians for the Holy Land

---

[8]   *De Civitate Dei*, lib. 18, cap. 45.

ended long ago, and still we have not seen any renewal of
Jerusalem, nor the devil and the false prophets thrown into
hell. For now, as even our adversaries affirm, the devil and
the false prophets greatly flourish.

Besides, God himself manifestly showed by means of
clear signs and wonders, both at Antioch in Syria, and on
other places, that he was pleased by that war.[9]

Next, St. Bernard, whom the same Bibliander calls a
saint in his chronicle, where he treats on the times of
Eugene III, was one of many authors of this war. For he
persuaded a multitude of French and Germans by words
and miracles to set out for that war, as he himself shows.[10]
The author of the life of St. Bernard writes that after the
battle was completed Bernard gave sight to a certain blind
man in testimony that the war he had preached was in the
name of the Lord.[11]

The sixth opinion is of the Centuriators, who teach that
Gog and Magog mean the kingdom of the Saracens or the
Turks.[12] Such an opinion is plainly opposed to that of
Bibliander and therefore, it is better or at least less bad. Yet
still, it is absolutely false. Gog will come in the end of his
years and will not endure for a long time, as is gathered
from John and Ezechiel. But the kingdom of the Saracens
began a long time ago and has endured for nearly a
thousand years, which is by no means a little while.

The seventh opinion is of St. Ambrose. He taught that
Gog represents the Goths, who had devastated many

---

[9] See William of Tyre, *de bello sacro*, lib. 6; Paulus Aemilius, *de rebus Francorum*, lib. 4.

[10] *De Consideratione*, lib. 2.

[11] *Vita B. Bernardi*, lib. 2, cap. 4.

[12] *Centur.* 1, lib. 2, cap. 4, col. 435.

provinces of the Roman people.[13] St. Jerome calls to mind
this opinion and says: "Whether it may be true or not, the
end of the battle will show."[14] And now rightly the end of
the battle shows that it was not true, since after the wars
of the Goths we saw neither a renewal of the Church nor
did all wars end.

The eighth opinion is of St. Jerome himself. While
commenting on chapter 38 of Ezechiel he saw the difficulty
of the matter and expressed it in the mystical sense on
heretics after he omitted the literal sense. For he would
have it that Gog, which in Hebrew means roof, signifies
heresiarchs who have the character of a roof; they are
elevated and proud. Magog, on the other hand, since it is
translated "from the roof," means those who believe
heresiarchs and are to them as a building is to its roof. This
opinion, provided it is received in a mystical sense, is very
true, but it is not literal. Ezechiel says that Gog is going to
come in the end of years and John says in Apocalypse 20
that after a thousand years the same Gog is coming.
(However, all Catholics understand the thousand years as
the whole time which is from the arrival of Christ even to
Antichrist.) Therefore, since Gog is not going to come until
the end of the world, and the heretics began in the
beginning of the Church while the Apostles were still alive,
it is properly certain that Gog does not literally mean
heretics. It must also be known that Jerome, when he says
Gog means roof and Magog means from the roof, did not
wish to say that Gog and Magog were the Hebrew for our
words roof and from the roof. Rather, he meant they are
almost the same. Properly in Hebrew roof is not Gog, but
Gag גג and for from the roof they do not say Magog, but

---

[13] *De fide*, lib. 2, cap. ult.

[14] *Quaest. Hebraicis in Gen.*, cap. 10.

Miggag מגנג.

The ninth opinion is of St. Augustine. He understands for Gog the devil, who is the character of a great roof, that is, of a great house in which many of the wicked inhabit; while for Magog he understands the army of Antichrist gathered from all the nations of the whole world.[15] Such an opinion without a doubt is the truest and must be embraced, insofar as it relates to Gog and Magog in the times of Antichrist. Both because all Catholic authors follow him, but also because everything which they say on Gog and Magog from Ezechiel and John rightly agree with Antichrist. For then, there will be truly the last and greatest persecution, and after it Jerusalem will be renewed, e.g. the Church will be glorified and no more wars are heard of. Insofar as he understands the devil for Gog it does not seem to be true. For John says the devil, being freed, is going to call Gog and Magog into battle; therefore, the devil is one thing, Gog is another.

Therefore, our opinion, which is the tenth, contains three things. Firstly, we assert that the battle of Gog and Magog is the battle of Antichrist against the Church, as Augustine rightly teaches. Secondly, we say it is probably quite true that Antichrist is signified by Gog while through his army, Magog. For Ezechiel perpetually calls Gog the prince, and Magog the land, or nation. Thirdly, we say it is probable that Gog is called by Magog, not the other way around, so that Antichrist should be called Gog, because he is the prince of the nation which is called Magog. Hence, the army of Antichrist is called Magog from the nation of Scythia not because it is certain to be made of Scythians, which the Jews mean by beyond the Caucasus and the Caspian Sea, but either because a great part of the army of

---

[15]   *De Civitate Dei*, lib. XX, cap. 11.

Antichrist will consist of barbarians arising from Scythia (such as Turks, Tartars, and others), or what I rather more believe, because it will be an immense army and very cruel. For those whom we wish to say are savage, we call Scythian.

Now, that Magog really means a Scythian nation is clear from Genesis 10, where we read that the second son of Japhet was called Magog, whereby it was called the region of Magog, which his posterity inhabited; which is Scythia as Josephus taught,[16] as well as St. Jerome.[17] This is the same as from the three sons of Cham, that is, Chus, Mizraim and Chanaan: Ethiopia was called Chus, Egypt was called Mizraim, and Palestine was called Chanaan; thus from the son of Japhet, Scythia was called Magog.

Moreover, when Ezechiel names Magog he regarded a nation denominated by Magog, the son of Japhet, because he adds as allies to it Gog and other nations denominated by other sons, or grandchildren of Japhet, such as Gomer, Togorma, Mosoch, Tubal, etc. Therefore, we conclude that the battle of Gog and Magog is the last persecution which Antichrist will excite against the Church in the whole world.

What Ezechiel says in chapter 38 is also not opposed to this, that the arms of Gog and Magog will be burned for seven years, since still it will be certain that after the death of Antichrist there will be but 45 days until the end of the world, as is gathered from Daniel. For Ezechiel does not speak literally, but figuratively as is the custom of prophets. He did not really mean that those arms would be burned for seven years, but that the slaughter would be so great that one could suffice for a very long time to keep the

---

[16] *Antiquit.*, lib. 1, cap. 11.

[17] *Quaest. Hebraicis in Genes.*, cap. 10.

fires going with spears and shields of the slain men, if one needed to.

One doubt remains, whether on account of the savage persecution of Antichrist the faith and religion of Christ must be throughly extinguished throughout the world. Domingo de Soto believes that it is going to happen: "The loss and defection of the whole world from that see will be a sign of the end of the world. ... After the faith has been extinguished through the defection from the Apostolic See, the whole world will be empty and then continue in vain. ... Mortals will become frightened, as their love shall be pestilent. Thence its glorification and pride which under the leadership of Antichrist will at length cause the city of God to shake."[18]

But, in my judgment, this opinion cannot be defended. For in the first place it is opposed to what Augustine says, that the Church is going to always be unconquered by Antichrist: "He will not desert his army which was called by the word 'camp'."[19] Next, it seems opposed to the Gospel, for we read in Matthew 16: "Upon this rock I will build my Church, and the gates of hell shall not prevail against it." But how will they not prevail, if they will utterly extinguish her? Likewise in Matthew 24, the Lord says on the ministers of Antichrist: "They will perform great signs, so that they will lead into error, and if it were possible, even the elect." There, the Lord meant the many chosen in that future time that will not allow themselves to be seduced by the miracles of Antichrist. Next, all writers who speak on the persecution of Antichrist, such as Ezechiel, Daniel, Paul, John and all the Fathers cited above, say that the victory of this war or persecution is

---

[18] *Sent.*, lib. 4, dist. 46, q. 1, artic. 1.

[19] *De Civitate Dei*, lib. 20, cap. 11.

going to be in the power of the Church. And the reasoning is evident. Who would believe that in this battle, in which the whole camp where God and the devil, Christ and Antichrist will fight, that God will be conquered by the devil, and Christ by Antichrist?

CHAPTER XVIII

The Absurdities of the Heretics are Refuted, in Which They not only try to Show, but Impudently Declare that the Roman Pontiff is Antichrist

LTHOUGH what we have treated up to this point on Antichrist could suffice, seeing that we have clearly shown that no place attributed to Antichrist in the divine Scripture agrees with the Supreme Pontiff, still so as to leave nothing wanting and because the impudence of our adversaries is so manifest, I propose briefly to refute that which Luther, Calvin, Illyricus, Tilman and Chytraeus assert trying to show that the Pope is the Antichrist.

1) Luther everywhere calls the Supreme Pontiff the Antichrist, and especially in his book *de Captivitate Babylonica,* in his work *Contra Execrabilem Bullam Antichristi,* in his assertion of articles, and in his book against Ambrose Catharinus.[1] Though he does this, only one argument can be found in all these books whereby he tries to prove this, namely in his assertion of article 27. He says: "Daniel foretold in the eighth chapter that Antichrist will be an impudent king by face, this is, as the Hebrew has it, powerful in regard to pomps and ceremonies of external works, meanwhile the spirit of faith is extinguished just as we saw fulfilled in so many religious orders, colleges, rites, vestments, deeds, churches, statues, rules and observances—and you can scarcely recite their number." And these same faces of Antichrist, as he calls them, he enumerates and profusely explains in his book against

---

[1] Translator's note: Lacelotto Politi, a Dominican canon lawyer.

Ambrose Catharinus on the vision of Daniel.

For all that, this argument of Luther errs in three places. First, in the very foundation, since the Hebrew word עז פנים (sha-panim)[2] means "robust in the face," and it is a Hebrew phrase that means a man with a smooth forehead who does not know how to be ashamed. For especially the Septuagint so renders it: ἀναιδὴς προσώπῳ, that is modest in the face. So also St. Jerome and Theodoret render it, and Francis Vatablus so explained it in the *Rules of Rabbis*: "Strong in face, that is he who does not blush, who has no shame."

Next, the same is gathered from Ezechiel 3: "The house of Israel has been rubbed clean in the forehead, and is hard of heart; behold I have given your face more vigor than their faces, and thy forehead is harder than theirs." The Hebrew for that is: "The house of Israel is robust in its forehead, and I gave your face to be more robust than theirs." The words have no other sense than this (as Jerome rightly explains): They are indeed impudent, but you shall not yield to their impudence. Although they boldly and without shame do wicked things, you boldly and without shame shall rebuke them. Since that is so, Luther should see to it lest he shall be impudent in face if he would have his interpretation be put before that of the rabbis, Theodoret, Jerome, the translators of the Septuagint and Ezechiel himself.

2) The argument of Luther goes astray because from this opinion, whatever at length he means, he does not rightly gather that the Pope is the Antichrist. Even if it were certain that Antichrist is going to be powerful in

---

[2] Translator's note: This is the Hebrew word as in the Ingolstadt and subsequent editions of the *Controversies*, but it is misspelled and we have not been able to discover the Hebrew word that Bellarmine intended.

pomps and external ceremonies, it is still not immediately gathered that Antichrist is whoever comes in pomps and external ceremonies. The logicians teach that nothing can be gathered from affirmative particulars. Otherwise Moses would be the Antichrist because he established so many ceremonies in Exodus and Leviticus that one can hardly begin to count them. And when the same thing is said about Antiochus, and in his figure of Antichrist, that understanding is perhaps enigmatic. If the reasoning of Luther would avail, it would follow that all who could answer the enigma are Antichrist. But that is certainly false and ridiculous.

3) Luther errs in attributing the institution of all orders and ecclesiastical ceremonies to the Roman Pontiff, when it is certain that a great many of these were established by the holy Fathers, not by the Roman Pontiff. The Greek Church has always had, and still has, monasteries, rites, observances and ceremonies which they received from St. Basil, St. Pachomius and the other Greek Fathers, not from the Roman Pontiff.[3] In the West also we have the orders of St. Benedict, St. Romuald, St. Bruno, St. Dominic, and St. Francis which, while approved by the Pope, were established and devised by these holy men with the teaching of the Holy Spirit. So, if orders pertain to the face of Antichrist, these holy Fathers must rather more be called Antichrist than the Pope.

I add, lastly, that the words of Daniel (except in regard to revealing Antichrist in his own time), agree more suitably to no man better than Luther. For he was impudent in his face above all, for as a priest and monk he openly married a consecrated virgin, when no example of such a thing can be shown in all of antiquity. Likewise, he

---

[3] See the books of Cassian in the *Institutes*, and the *Constitutions of St. Basil.*

wrote lies without number which have been recorded and published by many. John Cochlaeus writes in the acts of Luther for the year 1523, that in one book of Luther he noted fifty lies. From another Luther was found to have placed 874 lies. Next, how great was his impudence when, in his book against the Bull of Leo X, Luther dared to excommunicate his Pope when the universal Church adhered to him still? Who ever heard that a priest could excommunicate a bishop?

To be sure, the Council of Chalcedon abhorred the rashness of a certain Dioscorus, who, while presiding over the Second Council of Ephesus (that is, the robber council of Ephesis), presumed to excommunicate Pope Leo the Great. Yet, what comparison can there be between Dioscorus, the Patriarch of the second See, presiding in what was supposed to be a general council, and Luther, a simple monk writing in his cell? Nevertheless, leaving Luther, we come to Melanchthon.

CHAPTER XIX
The Trifles of the Smalchaldich Council of the Lutherans are Refuted

HERE is a little book extant on the power and primacy of the Pope, or the reign of Antichrist, published in the name of the Smalchaldich Council of the Lutherans, which seems to me to be the work of Melanchthon. At any rate, whoever wrote it, it has nothing but words and inane boasting. The author of the book says: "It is certain that the Roman Pontiffs, along with their members, defend impious doctrine and impious worship, and this plainly fits the mark of Antichrist in the rule of the Pope and his members." To this point we have seen the proposition, now let us hear the proofs: "For Paul, when describing Antichrist in his letter to the Thessalonians, calls him the adversary of Christ, extolling himself over everything which is called or worshiped as God, sitting in the temple just as God. Therefore, he speaks on someone ruling in the Church not on heathen kings; he calls this man the adversary of Christ because he is going to devise doctrine opposed to the Gospel and he will arrogate divine authority to himself."

Though all these things, even if they were true, would hardly impede us still, I ask on what foundation does this interpretation rest? Paul clearly says Antichrist is going to elevate himself over every god and is going to sit in the temple, not as a king or as a bishop, but plainly as God, and Chrysostom, Ambrose and the rest of the fathers interpreting this passage concur with this. Therefore, by what principle does he affirm without a witness or any reasoning that Antichrist is he who sits in the temple not as God, but as a bishop, and does not raise himself above every god, to such an extent that he not only worships God the Father, Son and Holy Spirit, but even prostrates himself before the Sacrament of the Eucharist in the sight of all, as well as before the tombs of the Apostles, martyrs, the cross and images of Christ and the saints, which the author himself, although impiously, usually calls foreign gods and idols? But let us see whether he can make this very thing fit the Pope.

"First, it is certain that the Pope rules in the Church and constituted this reign under the pretext of ecclesiastical authority and ministry. The pretext is these words: 'I give to you the keys'."

For certain he says that the Pope rules over the Church, but he does not prove it. On the other hand, we can show the contrary with little labor. One who rules suffers no superior, but the Pope professes that he is the vicar of Christ the King. And although in the whole house of God, and also in the whole kingdom of Christ he uses the fullest power, still this power is not in excess of the economy, rather it is the condition of a servant. For even Moses (as Paul says in Hebrews 3) "was faithful in the whole house of God," but just as a servant, while Christ is as a son in his own. But let us continue.

"Thereupon, the doctrine of the Pope is in many ways opposed with the Gospel and he arrogates to himself divine authority in three ways. First, because he takes for himself the right of changing the doctrine of Christ and the worship established by God, and wills his own doctrine and worship to be observed as though it were divine."

Likewise, he says this but does not prove it. Not only is this false, but it seems to be an impudent lie. Does he not know that in the Catholic Church the doctrine of Christ is taught by the mouth of all, and the worship cannot be changed not only by any man, but even by an angel, nor was there ever any question of whether what Christ taught or commanded should be believed or done. Yet it remains to be seen whether he or we interpret the doctrine and precepts of Christ better. In such a question he brings nothing other than his customary interpretation; but we bring the consensus of the Fathers, and of the Catholic Church, as well as decrees and customs. For we do not oppose the consensus of the Fathers and the decrees and customs of the Church (as he falsely boasts) let alone the Word of God, but only his interpretation and judgment. But let us hear the second proof.

"Secondly, because he takes power to himself not only to bind and loose in this life, but even the right over souls after this life."

Again, this is said but not proven. For the Supreme Pontiff does not take the right unto himself over dead souls. He does not absolve their sins or punishments by his own authority but only in a manner such as prayers of intercession, and he will also share the good works of the faithful with them. Moreover, prayers and fasting of the living benefit the dead, and especially the sacrifice of the Mass, as all the Fathers teach. On that matter we will dispute profusely elsewhere; in this place one testimony of St. Augustine will suffice. "It is without question that the dead are assisted by the prayers of the Holy Church and the salutary sacrifice, as well as almsgiving which is expended for their souls."[1] Still, let us go on.

"Thirdly, because the Pope refuses to be judged by the Church or by another and advances his authority in judgment of councils and of the whole Church. This is to make oneself God, to refuse to be judged by the Church or

---

[1]   Serm. 34.

by anyone."

Here also, he says two things that he cannot prove. For particularly by what Scriptures, what councils, by what criterion ought the Pope be judged by councils or the Church? For we read (that I might pass over many other things which were disputed in the previous book) that Christ said to Peter: "Feed my sheep."[2] We believe, it cannot be doubted, that the sheep must be ruled and judged by a shepherd, not the shepherd by the sheep. We also read that in Luke the Lord said to Peter: "Who do you think is the faithful and prudent steward, whom the Lord constituted over his household?"[3] We see in that passage a specific steward was proposed for the whole household of Christ, and certainly that he would rule it, not be ruled by it.

Still, perhaps someone would object that if that steward were wicked, in the end who will judge him if the steward is in charge of all but subject to none? That is why the Lord added immediately after: "What if that servant would have said in his heart, 'My Lord delays his coming,' and began to strike the servants and maidservants, to eat, drink and be drunk; the master of the servant will come on a day on which he hopes not, and at an hour which he does not know, and he will divide his lot and share it with infidels."[4] Who does not hear that there is a judge of that wicked steward whom the Lord constituted over his household? Christ does not say that he will be judged by a council, but the "Lord will come on a day he hopes not, etc." Therefore, the Lord reserves judgment for himself over the one he himself constituted over his whole household. Hence, the

---

[2] John 21:17.

[3] Luke 12:42.

[4] Luke 12:45-46.

Pope does not steal his authority from the judgment of councils and of the whole Church when he does not suffer himself to be judged by it. He cannot steal what was never given in the first place. Rather, councils duly gathered have never taken to themselves (outside the case of heresy), to pass judgment on the Supreme Pontiff. There is much to say on this matter in the proper place.

The second thing that he says and does not prove is that one makes himself God if he refuses to be judged by the Church or by anyone. For when he says "by anyone," he certainly understands any man; does Melanchthon not know that the Pope must be judged by Christ himself, and that he believes and professes this? By what arrangement does someone make himself God when he believes God must judge him?

Next, earthly kings attain judgment on earth in regard to matters of state; they recognize no one, and by his scheme, where he removes coercive power from bishops, these kings have no judge in ecclesiastical affairs. Will there not then be as many gods as there are kings? I do not think he is that insane that he would say this. Therefore, it remains that it is not true that one who would not be judged by any man thereby makes himself God.

Finally, he adds: "He defends such horrible errors and this impiety with supreme savagery, and he kills anyone who dissents."

Since he lies so impudently here, let him also, if he can, recognize that I myself who write this openly assert—and at that in the very city of Rome (and not without the Pope's knowledge)—that it is not lawful for the Pope to change Christ's doctrine, or worship, or establish new worship which should be held as divine, or which is opposed with the Gospel by any reasoning. I am not killed for that, nor do I suffer on that account. Without a doubt the Pope knows well that I speak the truth, but Melanchthon lies. Just the same he also adds a little after: "The doctrine on penance has been altogether twisted by the Pope and his members; for he teaches that sins are remitted on account of the dignity of our works; in like manner they never teach that sins are remitted by grace on account of Christ." These, however, are not our teachings but his lies. For we do not teach that, but altogether the contrary, as the Council of Trent clearly shows.[5] But enough has been said on this. Let us now turn to Calvin.

---

[5]   Sess. 6, ca. 5-8

CHAPTER XX

The Lies of Calvin are Refuted

OHN CALVIN, explaining 2 Thessal. 2: "He who extols himself over everything that is called God," says many things with great flamboyance, but proves nearly nothing. "Paul means by these words that Antichrist was going to take as his own what is of the one God, that he will raise himself above everything divine and every god, that he might lay at his feet all religion and the whole worship of God. ... Now whoever will have been informed by the Scripture, even if he be a boy of but ten years, will notice certain things which are especially proper to God and which, on the other hand, the Pope usurps to himself, and he need not expend much labor to recognize him [the Pope] as Antichrist." This shows wonderful promise!

But let us, at length, hear by what reasoning he shall prove what he proposes. Perhaps it will be of the kind that even a boy of ten years will not labor much to refute it: "The Scripture proclaims that God alone is the legislator[1] who can preserve and destroy,[2] one king whose office is to rule souls by his word; it makes the same one the author of all sacred things; it teaches that justice and salvation depend upon Christ alone; and it assigns the mode together with the reasoning. The Pope asserts that every one of these pertains to his right; and he boasts that what seems fit to him he binds upon consciences by means of laws and subjects them to eternal punishments. He

---

[1] Isaiah 33:22.

[2] James 4:12.

establishes Sacraments at his pleasure which are either new or corrupted from the ones which Christ had established, and he vitiates, nay more, altogether abolishes these so that in their place he substitutes the sacrileges that he had made. A foreign means of attaining salvation is devised that is altogether foreign to the Gospel. Lastly he does not hesitate to change the whole religion at a nod. What, I ask, is it to raise oneself over everything which is called divine if the Pope does not do it?"

Did I not say that Calvin says much, but proves little or nothing? For Calvin says all this, that the Pope boasts to bind men with laws upon their consciences as he sees fit, that he establishes new Sacraments but abolishes the old, that he devises a means of salvation foreign to the doctrine of the Gospel, that he changes all religion—but he does not prove any of it. In other words, for him to say something is to prove it; by equal reasoning to deny it ought to refute it.

Certainly, however, many of us are Catholic, and we obey the Roman Pontiff, the Vicar of Christ; we speak freely and without any injury to him that he is not allowed to bind men with any law he pleases, i.e. pernicious and wicked ones, neither can he establish new Sacraments nor corrupt or abolish the ones established by Christ, nor is he permitted to confect a means of salvation foreign to the doctrine of the Gospel, or overturn the Christian religion, or change it. We, in truth, more gladly say that we know he also thinks and says the same thing. For if he did not think so, if he thought he was allowed to fashion wicked laws, establish new Sacraments or abolish the old or do other things of this sort, how would he knowingly and willingly suffer us, who are in his power here in Rome more than in I know not what corner of the world, to teach the contrary?

But they will say the Pope does not say he is permitted to do these things, but still in reality he contends that he is by his deeds. Therefore, it should be proven that he has done any of these things. Otherwise, that is to assume what must be proven, which although customary for our adversaries, the logicians call "begging the question."

Next, Isaiah 33 and James 4, the only two passages of Scripture that Calvin advanced, do not impede our position in the slightest. For Isaiah and James say: "One is king, judge and our lawgiver;" certainly that is not opposed with those words of Proverbs: "Through me kings rule and makers of laws determine what is just."[3] And with these, the Psalm: "And now understand ye kings, you are taught to judge the earth."[4] Another six hundred passages could be added. Therefore, Isaiah and James in whatever way do not make God the one king, judge and lawgiver, but only by reason that he alone is so King, Judge and Lawmaker that he ought to render an account to no one since he depends upon no one. He will rule and judge and impose laws by his own authority, i.e. he does not receive authority from another. Lastly, that he alone in regard to execution can destroy and save, as James says, we attribute none of that to the Pope or any other princes.

---

[3] Proverbs 8:15.

[4] Psalm 2:10.

CHAPTER XXI
The Lies of Illyricus are Refuted

OW we turn to Illyricus. In a book which he wrote against the primacy of the Pope, he says: "But among our other arguments it ought to be the most solid, truly and clearly proven that in this time, the Pope teaches and defends impious doctrine and is himself the very person of Antichrist, and I repeat the reasons of this matter here. 1 John 2 defines that Antichrist is he who denies Jesus is the Christ. The Pope clearly does this, not by words but by deed. Messiah is the Hebrew, Christ the Greek; it is a divinely sent person that he should be a perpetual priest and king over the people of God. The office of the priest is to teach, pray, sacrifice, but it is for a king to rule and defend."

Let us see how he will prove the Pope has snatched up these offices from Christ, and what testimony and proofs he advances. Still, unless I am mistaken, we will only see inane words. Therefore, he continues thus: "The Pope has seized the priesthood from Christ; not only does he wish to be heard as the beloved son, but what is more, he and his pseudo-apostles advance another Gospel. Likewise, he substitutes other mediators in heaven between us and Christ who intercede for us in the presence of the Father by neglecting the severe judge, Christ. Likewise, because he substitutes infinite sacrificing priests in place of Christ, who pleased God on behalf of the human race, to whom he says the priesthood passed from Christ through Peter. Thereupon, he wills us to be saved through their spiritual merits and those of the saints."

157

See how Illyricus conquers us with the clear proofs of Scripture! What if we were to show that all these things were merely lies? For where, I ask, have you read that the Pope wishes to be given more authority than Christ? We deny it and say: Prove it. Rather, we see that supreme honor is given to the Scriptures by the Pope and he holds for heretics those who teach something against Scripture. Next, is it not clearly a lie that the Pope has established other mediators for Christ and wants them to intercede with God the Father while neglecting Christ? Does our litany not begin with *Kyrie eleison, Christe eleison*? Are not all the prayers of our Church, which we read in Mass or in the Divine Office directed to God and do they not end: "through Christ our Lord"? Do we not acknowledge the mediation and intercession of Christ when, whatever we ask from God, or if we desire the saints to be asked on our behalf, we ask entirely through the merit of Christ? We do not have saints in place of God or of Christ, but we ask from them that they might join their prayers with our own so that whatever we wish of God we might obtain more easily through Christ.

By equal reasoning it is a lie that the Pope substituted sacrificing priests for Christ. Neither would we say the priesthood of Christ has passed to sacrificing priests through Peter. He has not proved any of these things, nor will he ever prove them. There can be no doubt whether if you had some means you would advance it. But it is as we say, Christ, who is a priest forever, and lives always to intercede for us, offered himself once to God in a pleasing sacrifice by death on the cross, but now he offers himself again and again and again in the liturgy through the hands of the priests.

Just the same, although many in our time baptize, still

we read that: "This is he who baptizes in the Holy Spirit."[1] It does not follow that the office of baptizing passed from Christ to the priests, but that he is the one who always baptizes through the ministry of the priest; thus even though many priests today offer Christ in awe-inspiring mysteries, still, he is the primary priest and truly the high priest who through the ministry of all priests offers himself: "These works are not of human power. Who then in that supper consecrates, now also operates and perfects; we merely hold the rank of ministers."[2]

But I would gladly say to Illyricus, since all the ancient writers both Greek and Latin make mention of the sacrifice of the Eucharist and of the Christian priesthood (which no man denies unless he does not read), why at length does he attribute this to the Roman Pontiff, that he transferred the priesthood of Christ to sacrificing priests? But let us continue with the rest.

He adds in the last passage: "He wishes us to be saved through their spiritual merits, and of the saints." This is also a characteristic lie. Otherwise advance a place where the Pope will have said this. St. Peter says in Acts: "For we believe we are saved by the grace of our Lord Jesus Christ, just as even our Fathers were saved."[3] Nor do we acknowledge any other savior but Jesus Christ crucified who gave himself for the redemption for all.[4]

Hence, it cannot be denied that the merits and prayers of the saints benefit us according to their mode, unless one does not know or does not believe there is communication and connection among the members of the body of the

---

[1] John 1:33.

[2] St. John Chrysostom, homil. 83 in Matth.

[3] Acts 15:11.

[4] 1 Tim. 2:5-6.

Church. Although we will treat this matter in another place, it will suffice to add two testimonies here. St. Augustine says: "That we might be advised in that mode, should what we deserve so weigh us down that it seems we are not loved by God, we can relieve ourselves from it by the merits of those whom God loves."[5] He also repeats often in *City of God* that some obtained forgiveness by the merits of the saints.[6] This is what the Lord meant when he said: "Make unto yourselves friends from the mammon of iniquity, that when you falter, they might receive you in eternal dwellings."[7] St. Leo the Great says: "We believe and trust to obtain the mercy of God when we are oppressed by our own sins, that we are always, among all labors of this life in equal measure, in need of the help by the prayers of special patrons, we are raised up only by Apostolic *merits*."[8]

Moreover, although we do not customarily so speak, as Illyricus says, that we are saved through spiritual merits, still, if anyone were to so speak and mean by the merits of the saints we are helped to obtain salvation through Christ, he could be no more rebuked than the Apostle Paul, who said: "I am all things to all men that I might save all."[9] And the Apostle Jude, who speaks in a similar fashion said: "And indeed reprove those that have been judged, but save others, pulling them out of the fire."[10] That is enough on the priesthood of Christ.

Nevertheless, Illyricus continues: "He steals the

---

[5]   Quaest. 149 *in Exodum*.

[6]   *De Civitate Dei*, lib. XXI, cap. 27.

[7]   Luke 16:9.

[8]   Leo I, *serm. 1 de natali Apostolorum*, Bellarmine's emphasis.

[9]   1 Corinth. 9:22.

[10]   Jude 1:22-23.

kingdom from Christ, because he wishes to be head of the Church on earth, but in heaven he constitutes other helpers and saviors for us, to whom he bids us to flee when in misery. Therefore the Pope denies Jesus is the Christ."

First I ask where in the world the Pope, or any Catholic, calls the saints "saviors"? I add this: If he asserts that he is head of the Church under Christ, as his vicar and minister, which the Pope does, is that to deny Jesus is the Christ? By the same reasoning does anyone who is a viceroy, or affirms himself as the governor of some province, thereupon deny his master is king?

Next, if to turn to the saints as helpers is to deny Jesus is the Christ, how, I ask, did Paul not deny Jesus is the Christ when he said: "I ask you, brethren, through our Lord Jesus Christ and through the charity of the Holy Spirit, that you help me by praying for me to God, that I might be freed from the unbelievers who are in Judea."? [11] How did Basil the Great not deny Jesus is the Christ when, in his *Oration on 40 martyrs*, he said: "Anyone who is oppressed in narrow straits, let him flee to them; again who rejoices, let him pray to them; that he may be freed from evils; that he would endure to prosperous times"? I omit the remaining Fathers, as I fear lest we might search too much and discover who else denied Jesus is the Christ.

Still, Illyricus continues. "In Daniel 11, Antichrist is distinguished by a great many signs; first, that he will do what he wants, and the Pope does what is pleasing to him."

But when holy Daniel says of Antichrist, "He will do what he wishes," he means Antichrist will have no one greater than he, not even God. For it follows: "And will be lifted up against every God." Therefore, Antichrist will live for his own will in place of the law of God, and command and subordination. Certainly the Pope does not do this;

---

[11]   Romans 15:31.

rather he affirms that he is constrained by the law of God, and acknowledges Christ as his judge and superior.

Illyricus continues: "He confesses in canons[12] that he himself drags infinite souls with him into hell; still no man ought to say to him what he does? And the Gloss says the will of the Pope is held as the rule."

The Canon that begins *Si Papa* was not (as Illyricus falsely says) written by any Pope, but by St. Boniface, the bishop of Moguntium, Apostle of Germany and a martyr. He does not deny that the Supreme Pontiff, if he will have lived badly, must be corrected and also admonished by fraternal charity; rather, he denies that he can be convicted by authority and judged when he is the judge of every man. In those words which come before that canon (as is seen in the new edition of the decree), Boniface also calls the Roman Church the *Head* of all Churches with eloquent words, and affirms that the safety of the whole Church, after God, depends upon the safety of the Roman Pontiff.

I ask, therefore, from Illyricus, whether the teaching of St. Boniface, the apostle of the Germans, is true or not? For if it is not true, why object to us? If it is true, why does he not receive it? I will put the matter more plainly. If his teaching is not true, therefore, it is not true that the Roman Pontiff drags a great many souls with him to hell. What then? But if it is true, then the Roman Pontiff is truly the head of all Churches and the judge of all, judged by no one. For this reason, Illyricus should cease to argue with canons which can benefit him nothing. What pertains to the Gloss, Illyricus should know, that citation was either held by the Pope as false and thus purged from the new edition, or else it was never in that decree; I could not find it anywhere.

Illyricus goes on: "Secondly (Daniel) says that he will lift himself above God. The Pope did that as is clear from

---

[12] Dist. 40, *si Papa*.

the foregoing. Likewise, because he wishes to make himself heard more than God, blaspheming he loudly proclaims the Scripture the font of all heresy, schism, ambiguity and obscurity, etc."

It would behoove him to at least relate the words of Daniel faithfully. It does not say he will lift himself above God, but "he will be lifted against every God." And below: "Nor will venerate gods because he will rise against all of them." This very clearly shows the Pope has nothing in common with Antichrist, since Antichrist will worship no gods but the Pope worships the one God, Father, Son and Holy Spirit. Not only that, but if we were to believe Illyricus then he openly worships as many gods as there are saints in heaven and images on earth, not to mention relics under the earth.

Moreover, when he adds: "The Pope loudly declares the Scriptures are the font of heresies and schisms," I have certainly never read that in the writings of any Pope; but I have heard the word of Luther, that Scripture is the book of heretics.[13] If that were received in the right sense then I do not see why it would be duly condemned. For St. Hilary also, in his last book on councils, shows that a great many heresies were born from bad understanding of Scripture. Tertullian also boldly stated: "Nor am I trying to say that the Scriptures themselves were so arranged by the will of God as to furnish materials for heretics when I read 'there must be heresies,' which could not exist without the Scriptures."

Not only does the Pope very truly teach that there is ambiguity and obscurity in a great many passages of Scripture, but so also do all the Fathers. Even Luther himself, whether he wished to or not, was compelled to

---

[13]   Luther, in a preface to the history that happened in Stasfort, in the year 1536.

affirm this when he wrote in a preface to the Psalms: "I would not have it presumed by any man in my regard that I have done what still none of the saints or the most learned could furnish, i.e. to teach and understand the Psalter in its legitimate sense in all places. It is enough for some men to have understood some things for their part, but the Spirit has reserved many things to himself so that we would always have students. It only shows many things so as to attract, and hands down many things to influence. ... I know that anyone who would dare to profess that he had perfect understanding of one book of Scripture in all its parts would be guilty of the most impudent temerity." Luther also writes the same thing in his book *de Conciliis et Ecclesia*, pag. 52. Does he not clearly affirm that he, with great sweat, sought the true and genuine teaching of Scripture? And, at length, are there not so many versions of Scripture, so many interpretations, so many different sects among our adversaries; why do they shout, on the other hand, how ambiguous and obscure the Scripture is?

"Third, [Daniel] says that things will go well for him [Antichrist] until the wrath of God shall put an end to them. The Pope oppressed as he willed both kingdoms and innumerable churches with his tyranny and impiety."

And this is the reason by which the author proves his case? Could not someone say what states and which churches the Roman Pontiff has oppressed? What if we were to show the contrary, that this mark of the Pope were plainly contrary to this third mark of Antichrist? In that time, in which according to Illyricus, the Pope began to be Antichrist, not only did his rule not increase, but in fact it decreased all the more. In the time of Leo the Great, that is, one hundred and fifty years before our adversary says Antichrist was born, the Roman Pope presided over as many nations as there were boundaries of the Roman

Empire. For he thus writes: "Through the holy See of Blessed Peter, Rome was made head of the world; you preside more broadly in divine religion than earthly domination. Although by many victories the authority of your rule increased, you conferred it over land and sea; still what bellicose labor has subdued for you is less than what Christian peace has added."[14] And Prosper of Aquitaine says:

> Rome, the See of Peter, which for pastoral honor
> Was made head of the world,
> Whatever she does not possess by arms
> She holds by religion.[15]

Yet afterwards, while Antichrist was ruling (as Illyricus would have it) the Roman See little by little lost Africa, the greater part of Asia and all of Greece. In our own times they cry out that Antichrist is raging, yet all his affairs go so well that he has lost a great part of Germany, Sweden, Norway, all Denmark, a good part of England, France and Switzerland, Bohemia and part of the Balkans. Therefore, if things going well is a mark of Antichrist, it is not the Pope, who has lost so many provinces, but Luther, who by preaching carnal freedom has seduced so many people and for whom things go so well that from a private monk he became prophet of the whole of Germany; and just as the Pope evades it, he rightly can be called Antichrist. Nevertheless, continue.

"Fourthly, Daniel says 'he will have no care of the God of his Fathers.' This is truly said about the Pope, as we clearly proved above from the passage of John."

And we more clearly disproved it in the same place.

---

[14]   Serm. 1 de natali Apostolorum.

[15]   Liber *de ingratis.*

"Fifthly, he says he will have no care for the love of women: but the Pope became celibate both by instructing celibacy to his own, and by his homosexual lusts."

Here, I omit to say with what temerity Illyricus dares to say these things. Meanwhile, he has a simple task; either he could prove what he says or he cannot. I will not omit that the words of Daniel, although they sound this way in the Greek text, still in the Hebrew source are plainly contrary in the opinion of St. Jerome, who rendered the verse: "And he will be in lust for women." And although the Hebrew words רעל חמדת נשים (re-kal ke-me-dat na-shis), only mean reeling from lust for women, they also do not have any other words joined to them whereby it could be understood whether it will be or not be Antichrist that will lust after women. Still there are two conjectures which the version of St. Jerome makes more probable.

1) It is certain that Antiochus, whom Daniel is literally speaking about, was exceedingly addicted to the love of women: "Antiochus," Jerome says, "is said to have been very lustful and so greatly disgraced the royal majesty through foul deeds and corruption, that he publicly had relations with mimes and harlots, and satisfied his lust in the presence of the people."[16] If this is so, how believable is it that Daniel was going to speak about such a king that will not be lustful for women?

2) Another conjecture is that since Antichrist is going to come as the Messiah of the Jews, and the Jews await a multitude of wives from the Messiah, apart from other goods, it is not in any way probable that Antichrist is going to command or praise celibacy.

Lastly, I add that if it is a mark of Antichrist that he will proclaim celibacy, then not only the Pope, but all the

---

[16] Comment. huius loci.

Fathers and even the Apostles themselves were Antichrists. For (that I might pass over the rest which will be advanced in its proper place) listen to what the Fathers of the II Council of Carthage say, in canon 2 of that council: "All are pleased that bishops, priests and deacons who confect the Sacraments ought to abstain from wives as guardians of chastity, that what the Apostles taught and antiquity itself preserved, we also would safeguard." But let us continue.

"Sixth, Daniel says that he will worship the god Moazim, and with gold and silver, which he did, while he placed his whole piety in it, so that many wonderfully splendid temples were built and rested upon every kind of precious ornament and songs would resound."

Many things were written above on the god Moazim, where we showed that he is either Antichrist himself or the devil whom Antichrist will secretly worship. But it seems to me that our Illyricus makes Jesus Christ the god Moazim, which is an intolerable blasphemy. For all the temples which the Roman Pontiffs have splendidly built and adorned with gold and silver are consecrated to Christ our God, and no man can be said to not know that. If, therefore, the one who is worshiped in temples of this kind is the god Moazim who does not see that Christ himself would be the god Moazim? Moreover, the building and adorning of temples did not begin in the year 666, the year our adversaries would have it that Antichrist appeared, but nearly three hundred years earlier.

Listen to Eusebius (from Ruffinus' version): "From that fact joy was infused over us as if by a divine gift, especially at the sight of these places which a little before were destroyed by the treachery of the impious tyrants, that were now brought back to life with a more glorious construction, and high temples rose even higher for the humble assemblies."[17] St. Cyril of Jerusalem also says: "These who are now kings built this holy Church of the Resurrection, in which we are now, clothing it with silver and gold from their piety, and they made it splendid with silver monuments."[18]

See, if you will, the magnificence of the temples of Christians and the splendor of the vessels of the Church in Eusebius's *Life of Constantine*,[19] and Gregory of Nyssa;[20] Gregory Nazianzenus;[21] Chrysostom;[22] Cyril of Alexandria;[23] Damasus;[24] Ambrose;[25] Jerome;[26] Augustine;[27] Paulinus;[28] Prudentius in a hymn on St. Lawrence and Procopious in a book on the buildings of Justinian. Certainly, they all lived before the times of Antichrist, and still they witness that in each age their buildings were full of the ornaments of Christians, as we see these now, and they are beyond compare.

"Seventh, Daniel says that Antichrist will enrich his friends; the Pope has done that."

Clearly he so enriched John of Eck, John Cochlaeus, John Fisher of Rochester, Latomus, Driedo, Tapper, Pedro

---

[17]   *Hist. Eccles.*, lib. 9, cap. 10.

[18]   *Catechesi* 14.

[19]   *Vita Constantini*, lib. 3 et 4.

[20]   *In oratione de sancto Martyre Theodoro.*

[21]   Orat. 1 *in Iulianum.*

[22]   Hom. 66 *ad populum Antiochenum.*

[23]   *De recta fide ad reginas.*

[24]   *Vita Sylvestri.*

[25]   *De officiis*, lib. 2, cap. 21.

[26]   *In comment.* cap. 8 *Zachariah.*

[27]   *In Psalm* 113.

[28]   *Natali tertio Sancti Felicis.*

de Soto and so many other learned men, who, although they labored for days and nights to refute the frenzies of our adversaries, still, they received not even a penny from the Roman Pontiff. Although they expected no reward from men, they labored chiefly for the glory of God. But if the Roman Pontiff allots priestly opulence to cardinals and bishops, it is not as much that he believes they must be enriched as the piety of the faithful, who donate wealth to this purpose.

Illyricus continues: "Paul places five marks of Antichrist in 2 Thessalonians 2. 1) That he will sit in the temple of God. The Pope does this. He, by styling himself vicar of Christ, reigns over the consciences of men. For if he were to profess that he is the enemy of Christ, as the Mohammadans, he would be outside the Church."

But Paul does not only say Antichrist is going to sit in the temple of God (for every bishop sits in the temple of God), but he explains in what manner he is going to sit in the temple, showing himself ὅτι ἐστὶν Θεὸς. The Pope, on the other hand, by Illyricus' own testimony, makes himself the vicar of God, not God himself. A vicar of God cannot be God unless he would fabricate lesser gods as well as greater ones. Thereupon, I ask, if the Pope is not outside the Church, as he says in this passage, and hence is within the Church, where, I ask, is Illyricus with his own? Is he outside the Church? For the Church is one, and the Pope sits in it. He who is not in it, is in no Church at all. But let us hear the rest.

"2) The fact that Paul says that now a great mystery is worked: I think it looks to the fact that the bishop of Rome, a little later, would begin to raise his head above that of others."

Without a doubt, as we wrote briefly above, following Nicholas Sanders who had already seen and written this very thing, Illyricus would make St. Peter the Antichrist, but Christ to be Simon Magus or Nero to be Christ. For Paul did not say the mystery of iniquity will be worked a little later, but was being worked in his time. Why, if this mystery pertains to the Roman Pontiff, is it necessary to pertain to St. Peter and if St. Peter, (the mind shudders to think and the hand fears to write) was the Antichrist, who does not see that Simon Magus and Nero, the enemies of St. Peter, were Christ and God? Let Illyricus have Gods and Christs of this sort for himself; we will not envy him.

"3) What Paul says, that Antichrist is going to come with characteristic lies, which the Pope has done, as experience witnesses.

4) That God will permit the efficacy of illusion: this manifestly happens in the papacy. For by far we believed the Pope more strongly than God."

We have already treated on the miracles of Antichrist above (chapter 15) and what Illyricus says is "from experience" is a very impudent lie. The Popes have never done either true or false miracles (not in this age nor in a previous one), whereby Antichrist is said to principally rule. What he adds on the efficacy of illusion, anyone should see how easily this has been twisted into an adverse meaning. What greater efficacy of illusion can be contrived than that in our time some are discovered who prefer to trust two or three apostates than the universal Church, all councils and all the Fathers, who apart from admirable doctrine and outstanding sanctity of life, are glorified with many miracles?

Moreover, what Illyricus advances in his fifth mark from St. Ambrose was refuted above in the second proof, in which we showed that Antichrist has not yet come.

Lastly, Illyricus adds a little from the epistle to

Timothy: "In the last times many will leave the faith.[29] The Pope denies there is another faith apart from the historic one. They attend impostor spirits; the Pope proves all things by visions of spirits and souls. They forbid marriage, the use of food each of these from the Pope is very true and well known."

But, my good man, the Pope learned there is one faith from Paul; you seem to have learned from there something besides one faith; the Apostle says to the Ephesians: "One God, one faith, one Baptism."[30] Paul never defined this one faith as a trust resting upon the promise and Word of God, as you define it.[31] But he said to the Romans: "This is the word of faith which we preach, because if you shall confess the Lord Jesus in your mouth and will believe in your heart that God raised him from the dead, you will be saved."[32] He also said to the Hebrews: "By faith we believe the world was arranged by the Word of God."[33]

Who does not know that it pertains to sacred history that Christ rose from the dead and the ages are suited to the Word of God? Still, we do not call the one, only and true faith with which we certainly believe whatever God deigned to reveal by the Apostles and prophets historic faith, but Catholic faith. For we leave novelties of names to our adversaries.

What he adds, that the Pope proves all things by visions of spirits and souls, I do not know what spirit revealed to him. For to confirm those things which pertain to the state of souls, we apply something from apparitions

---

[29]   1 Timothy 4:1.

[30]   Ephesians 4:5.

[31]   Cent. 1, lib. 2, cap. 4, col. 262.

[32]   Romans 10:9.

[33]   Hebrews 11:3.

of souls and from the approved writings of ancient authors. Such is what Eusebius writes on the apparition of St. Potamina[34] and that which St. Augustine relates on the apparition of St. Felix Nolan.[35] On the other hand, I do not know who ever advanced visions of Catholic souls to prove dogmas. But that is not his first lie.

What he advances in the last place on the prohibition of foods and spouses is easily refuted by St. Augustine: "So, again, if you were to encourage virginity just as the apostolic doctrine does, 'He who gives in marriage does well, and he who gives not in marriage does better;' if you taught that marriage is good, and virginity better, as the Church teaches (which is truly Christ's Church), the Holy Spirit would not have heralded you as forbidding marriage. What a man forbids he says is evil, but he does not do so when he places something better before a good.... You see, then, that there is a great difference between exhorting to virginity by proposing it as the better of two good things, and forbidding to marry by denouncing the true purpose of marriage; between abstaining from food as a symbolic observance, or for the mortification of the body, and abstaining from food which God has created for the reason that God did not create it. In one case, we have the doctrine of the prophets and apostles; in the other, the doctrine of lying devils."[36] It is not necessary to add anything.

Illyricus concludes: "Therefore, it is certain from these clear signs that the Pope is himself the true Antichrist, about whom the Scriptures prophecy."

But perhaps he would more suitably conclude in this

---

[34]　*Hist. Ecclesi.* lib. 6, cap. 5.

[35]　Lib. *de cura pro mortuis*, cap. 16.

[36]　*Contra Faustum*, lib. 30, cap. 6.

way: Therefore it is certain from these clear lies, that Illyricus is one of his precursors, whom the holy prophet Daniel long ago foretold would have an impudent mouth.

CHAPTER XXII
The Ineptitude of Tilman is Refuted

ILMAN HESH wrote a book with the title *de Antichristo* that he subtitled "On six-hundred errors of the Popes" (which ought to be titled On six-hundred lies of the Lutherans). In it, he embraces four errors. Thus he says:

"The Popes say that Antichrist is going to come from Babylon from the tribe of Dan."[1]

Thanks are in order for Tilman, who teaches this is of ancient and holy Popes. If they are Popes who say Antichrist is going to come from the tribe of Dan, then certainly the Popes are Irenaeus, Hippolytus, Ambrose, Augustine, Prosper, Theodoret, Gregory, Bede, Arethas, Rupert, Anselm and Richard: all these, as we showed above,[2] teach in a common consensus that Antichrist is going to be born from the tribe of Dan. Still, we continue with Tilman.

"Secondly, the Papists deny that the Roman Pontiff, with his fellowship, are the true Antichrist, although it is proved and shown by very strong and clear testimonies of the divine word."

But we do not yet see these testimonies, nor are they extant in our Hebrew, Greek or Latin Bibles. For that which he advances as testimony for his side does not even name the Roman Pontiff.

"Thirdly, they teach Antichrist is only going to reign

---

[1] *Compendium Theologiae* lib. 7, cap. 8

[2] Chapter XIII.

for three and a half years."

Here, immortal thanks are due to Tilman, because he affirms that not only all the Fathers, but even the Prophet Daniel and John the Evangelist are Papists. And he thus duly spares me his and his own, by which he reserves merely the dregs of the Scriptures, having abolished all learned and approved Fathers to the Papists. Please see what we taught above (chapter 8) and one will find those who taught this with eloquent words, whom Tilman affirms are Papists for teaching it, namely Irenaeus, Hippolytus, Cyril, Jerome, Augustine, Theodoret, Primasius, Aretha, Bede, Anselm, Richard, Rupert and even Daniel and John.

"Fourthly, they teach Antichrist is going to be killed on Mt. Olivet."

And here also he makes great men into Papists. Accordingly, Antichrist must be killed on Mt. Olivet, as St. Jerome gathers from Daniel and Isaiah.[3] Theodoret also, writing in the same place, even if he does not name Mt. Olivet, he affirms Antichrist must be killed not far from Jerusalem. But we shall see by what arguments he refutes the aforesaid errors. For he immediately adds the antidote in these words:

"The papist trifles on Antichrist that rest upon no testimony of Sacred Scripture must be rejected and detested. Jerome rightly says that he who does not place authority in Scripture is condemned by the same levity whereby he asserts something. And Paul warns that we should beware of the traditions of men.[4] I say this, however, lest anyone would impose upon you with false reasoning, etc. Likewise: 'See lest anyone would deceive

---

[3] *In comment.* cap. 11 *Danielis.*

[4] Coloss. 2:8.

you by philosophy, etc.' It must be sought from the Word of God what is thought about Antichrist, such as in 1 John 2. 'Who is a liar but he who denies Jesus is the Christ? This is the Antichrist.' Likewise, 2 Thess. 2, 'The man of sin and son of perdition will raise himself over every God, etc.' Likewise Matth. 24, 'Pseudochrists will arise, and Pseudoprophets, and they will give signs, etc.' Daniel 11: "And he will make offering to the god Moazim,' and in Apocal. 17: 'And I saw a woman drunk on the blood of the saints and from the blood of the martyrs of Jesus.' From these Sacred Scriptures, what the Christian faith holds about Antichrist, whom Christ and the Apostles foretold is coming, appears crystal clear in its testimonies. Since they are more clearly brought into the light, each individual mark agrees more clearly with the Roman Pontiff, so there should be no doubt that the Roman tyranny is the worst Antichrist."

It will not be tiresome, I believe, if we recall these cruder arguments to a syllogism and thence conclude the confutation of the clear errors above. Therefore the first error is refuted. The trifles of Popes, because they rest upon no testimony of Scripture, must be rejected and detested. But the Word of God declares: "He who denies Jesus is the Christ, he is Antichrist."[5] Therefore, it is an error to say Antichrist is coming from the tribe of Dan.

The second error is thus confuted. As Jerome rightly says, whatever has no authority in Scripture is condemned by the same levity whereby it is asserted. But Paul says: "the man of sin, and son of perdition will raise himself over every God."[6] Therefore the Papists err when they deny the Pope is the Antichrist.

---

[5] 1 John 2:22

[6] 2 Thes. 2:3-4.

Thus the third, and more powerfully because it is from two Scriptures; St. Paul says, "I say this, lest they place false arguments upon you, etc."[7] And there will rise "Pseudochrists and pseudoprophets, and they will give signs, etc."[8] Therefore it is an intolerable error of the Popes when they say that Antichrist will rule for three and a half years.

The last and strongest of all because it is from three Scriptures. Paul warns: "See lest anyone deceive you with philosophy, etc."[9] Antichrist will make an offering to the god Moazim,[10] and John saw a woman drunk on the blood of the saints.[11] Therefore, the Papists err by the whole heaven when they say Antichrist is going to be killed on Mount Olivet.

Candid reader, forgive me for treating Tilman so ridiculously. Yet the impudence of the man compels me, since he has nothing worthy by way of refutation; but after writing such nonsense he still boasts as if he offered proofs as certain and as clear as in Mathematics.

---

[7] Coloss. 2:8.

[8] Matt. 24:24.

[9] Coloss. 2:8.

[10] Daniel 11:38.

[11] Apoc. 17:6.

CHAPTER XXIII
The Lies of Chytraeus are Refuted

AVID CHYTRÆUS takes up in his commentary on the Apocalypse a vision of John where, as the fifth angel blows a trumpet, a vast star was seen to fall from heaven to earth, to which was given the key of the well of the abyss. After that a dense smoke was seen to rise from the abyss that darkened the sun and the air. Lastly, some strange locusts were seen to advance from the smoke; a little after they bore before themselves the appearance of horses, lions, scorpions and armored men.[1] Chytraeus explains that he thought this vision corresponded to the Roman Pontiff, and would also have it so thought by others when he says: "There is no doubt that this vision describes Antichrist, or the order of the Roman Papacy."

He also teaches that this vision begins in the year 600, and that star falling from heaven was Gregory the Great, the Roman Pontiff; his successors are those who abandoned the keys of the kingdom of heaven and received the keys of the well of the abyss. The smoke advancing from the well is the corruptions of doctrine and various traditions of the Roman Pontiffs. Next, he would have it that the swarms of locusts are bishops, clergy, monks; and to dissipate that smoke he proposes that the antithesis of pontifical doctrine is the evangelical doctrine, which is Antichristian opposed to Christian, and embraces twelve articles, as if it were another Apostolic Creed.

---

[1]   Apocalypse 9:1-11.

179

But this opinion can easily be refuted. 1) It rests upon no witness. Amongst the Fathers who interpreted this verse, such as Arethas, Bede, Primasius, Anselm, Rupert and others on this place, the star which fell from heaven represents the devil, not some bishop. In Isaiah it is said about the Devil: "How did you fall from heaven, O Lucifer, who rose in the morning?"[2] And because the devil fell much earlier than John's Apocalypse, the Fathers note that John did not say I saw a star falling from heaven, but "I saw the star that had fallen from heaven to the earth." For John saw that star that already was on earth, which formerly had shined with the brightest light in heaven. It very suitably corresponds to the Devil, just as what follows: "And the key of the well of the abyss was given to him." As Christ has and shares the keys of the kingdom of heaven with his own and rules over the minds of the faithful and the pious, so the Devil has the key of the well of the abyss and rules over the sons of infidelity; he is everywhere called in the Scripture: "the prince of Darkness; the prince of this world; god of this age."[3] He is also the one who, with God's permission, sends out the smoke of errors from the well and new swarms of locusts, that is heresiarchs with their armies, in nearly every age against the boundaries of the Church.

2) The opinion of Chytraeus is opposed to what John says in this same chapter on the sixth angel, and the sixth persecution. St. John describes six persecutions of heretics through the trumpets of the six angels, which were going to come from the time of the Apostles even to the end of the world. And even Chytraeus is not far off in that he understands by the first trumpet the heresy of the

---

[2] Isaiah 14:12.

[3] John 12:31 and 14:30; 2 Cor. 4:4; Ephes. 6:12; Colos. 1:13 and other places.

Ebionites, which was roused in the time of the Apostles. For the second trumpet he understands the heresy of the Gnostics that came after it; for the third the heresy of Paul of Samosata and his followers as well as the Arians; the fourth heresy is of the Pelagians, who were later than all the previous heretics.

Moreover, if through the fifth trumpet the persecution of the Roman Antichrist is understood, which all agree is the last persecution, then what shall we understand by the sixth trumpet? Chytraeus responds that the sixth trumpet signifies the persecution of Muhammad and the Turks. But this is not said rightly, both because the Muslims are not heretics but pagans and because the persecution of Muhammad will not follow that of Antichrist but will precede it, just as we think, or it will take place at the same time, as Chytraeus says. Therefore, Chytraeus is compelled to confound the fifth trumpet with the sixth, when still he related the others to different times. Catholics understand the sixth trumpet better; it is the persecution of Antichrist which truly will be the last and most fierce; but through the fifth some exceedingly pernicious heresy which will nearly precede the times of Antichrist. Yea, many guess with great probability it will be the Lutheran heresy.

3) But Chytraeus errs by the whole heaven when he teaches that St. Gregory was the star falling to earth, since St. Gregory, if any trust can be placed in historians, did not fall from heaven to earth but ascended from earth to heaven. He went from a judge to a monk, from a monk he was made a bishop; he never went back from the episcopacy to his magistracy, or from a monk back to the world. This is the same as what St. Basil, Gregory Nazianzen and John Chrysostom did amongst the Greeks, and Martin, Paulinus, and Augustine among the Latins, who went from seculars to monks, and were thereafter

made bishops. No one ever said on that account that they fell from heaven to earth. Next, Gregory was second to none in regard to continence, sobriety and the love of heavenly things, but in humility he excelled all; and still Chytraeus would so boldly say that he fell from heaven, that is, from heavenly life to earth, nay more to an earthly life full of carnal delights.

Even Luther called Gregory a saint[4] and Luther followed Theodore Bibliander[5] in raising Gregory with the greatest praise; he said that the degree in which he excelled in zeal for piety and doctrine can be seen in his books, which is very true. For his writings breathe an admirable sanctity.

What he adds on the smoke from the well is no less vain. He interprets it as the corruption of doctrine introduced into the Church by Gregory and his successors. Yet, Gregory changed nothing which pertains to doctrine, instead what pertains to rites and discipline. He corrected many things which had crept in through abuse; he restored many things which had been forgotten by the negligence of time. Just so, he established a few new things, and those by mature counsel, as can be recognized both from the four books on his life, written by John the Deacon, and from his epistle where he explains the nature of the rites which he restored or instituted.[6] This matter will become especially clear if we review the very antithesis of evangelical and pontifical doctrine which Chytraeus proposes, not to mention by which he more often loses readers afterward.

---

[4] *In supputatione temporum.*

[5] Tab. 10 *Chronol.*

[6] 63. lib. 7.

I.

ON THE TRUE RECOGNITION AND INVOCATION OF GOD.

The Gospel teaches that only one God must be invoked and worshiped, just it is commanded to be done in his word. All trust in our salvation must be placed in the goodness and mercy of God alone. The Popes command men to invoke not only the true God, but also dead men or saints, to seek aid and help in perils and to wait for it, etc. This is plainly from a heathen custom; they bind the invocation and worship of God to certain statues, and thence if they come to this or that statue with invocation, God will be more merciful than to others.

Because we treat copiously on these controversies, which are touched upon in this *Antithesis*, in different places, here we will only show briefly that doctrine that Chytraeus calls "pontifical" is neither opposed with the Word of God nor began in the time of St. Gregory.

The Word of God teaches that only one God must be worshiped and invoked with that invocation and adoration which is due to God alone (who is also a jealous God should we hold a creature for a creator). Nevertheless, the same Word of God commands us to honor more excellent creatures, even that we might invoke some, but not as gods, rather as beloved members of God's family. Just the same, kings suffer if they would see royal honors conferred upon their servants, but they rejoice when they see the same servants honored and observed. David says, "Adore[7]

---

[7] Translator's note: We must draw the reader's attention to the fact that in Latin, terms like "worship" and "adore" are used in regards to the Blessed Virgin and saints, with the distinction that it is given with *dulia*, a Greek word indicating a lower level of dignity, whereas

the footstool of his feet."[8] and Job says: "Call, if there is one to respond to you, then turn to one of the saints."[9] For that reason Abdias, a great and holy man, adored Elijah prostrate on the ground.[10] And the sons of the prophets when they heard the spirit of Elijah had passed to Elisha, coming they "adored him prostrate."[11] And the Apostle Paul implored the prayers of Christians for nearly all individuals, that through these he would be liberated from many dangers. No other reasoning can be given why it would decrease the honor due to God, if we were to demand from the souls of the saints to pray for us to God, just as it is not diminished if we will ask the same thing from the living.

Thereupon, St. Ambrose, who is 200 years earlier than St. Gregory, still so speaks in his book on widows: "The angels must be implored, who were given to guard us; the martyrs must be beseeched, of whom the pledge of the body seems to us to claim patronage. We are not ashamed to employ them as intercessors in our infirmity."

Moreover, we do not assign worship and invocation to statues of the saints, to memorials of the martyrs, and the remaining religious monuments any differently than God did to the sanctuary or to the temple of Solomon. Even if God hears us everywhere, and we can lift up our hands to God in every place, still, it is not without a reason that the

---

adoration with *latria* is given to God alone. In English this is generally accomplished with "veneration" and "worship", but we are hesitant to constitute ourselves the correctors of Bellarmine's Latin.

[8] Psal. 98 (99):5.

[9] Job 5:1.

[10] 3 Kings (1 Kings) 18:7.

[11] 4 Kings (2 Kings) 2:15.

Holy Spirit[12] and Christ call the temple of God the house of prayer.[13] Nor is it without reason that the most pious emperor Theodosius (as meanwhile I might pass over a great many examples from antiquity) encompassed every place of prayer with the Priests and the people; before the reliquaries of martyrs and the Apostles they laid down prostrate on a rug and begged their faithful assistance from the saint's intercession. And certainly Theodosius who did this, and Ruffinus who wrote it[14] preceded St. Gregory by at least two hundred years.

II
On the Office and Benefits of Christ

The Gospel teaches that eternal life and remission of sins be given on account of the unique and only Son of God, our Lord Jesus Christ, crucified, died and resurrected for our sake, not for any work or merits of ours. And indeed, this honor is proper to God alone, as is said in Isaiah 43: "I am, I am he who blots out iniquities." Likewise: "There is no salvation in any other." The Popes teach the contrary, not on account of the merits of Christ alone, but partly on account of Christ, and partly on account of our contrition, obedience or good works, that we are justified and saved, etc.

Catholic doctrine does not hold that sinners will be justified partly by Christ and partly by their works, as if their works would merit anything without Christ. Accordingly, we distinguish three kinds of works. One

---

[12]   Isaiah 56:7.

[13]   Matth. 21:13.

[14]   Lib. 2 *hist. Eccl.* cap. 33.

type is done from the strength of nature alone without faith and the grace of God. Concerning these, we plainly declare with the Apostle that a man is not justified from works but from faith, and if someone would be justified from works of this sort he would have glory, but not before God, as St. Paul says about Abraham.[15] Therefore, there is no controversy on these works, even if here and there it is attributed to us that we teach works are meritorious without the faith of Christ, which is an impudent lie.

The second type of works proceed from faith and the grace of God which disposes one to reconciliation with God and remission of sins. Of this kind are prayer, almsgiving, fasting, sorrow for sins and others. We do not say such works are meritorious from the justice of the reconciliation itself, but on the contrary we hear what was said at the Council of Trent,[16] that men are justified by grace because neither faith nor the works which precede justification merit it, but from justice, as if justification were due to works of this sort. Still, we affirm these works themselves, insofar as they proceed from faith and divine assistance, are divine works and merit in that manner, *i.e.* obtain remission of sins. Even if one would not concede it, nevertheless he concedes the Word of God. Why is it that Ezechiel says: "And when the evil man turns himself away from the wickedness that he has done and does judgment, and justice: he shall save his soul"?[17] Why does Daniel say, "Redeem your sins with almsgiving"?[18] Why does Jonah say: "God saw their works (fasting and hairshirts) and

---

[15] Romans 4:2.

[16] Sess. 6, cap. 8.

[17] Ezechiel 18:27.

[18] Daniel 4:24.

pitied them"?[19] Why does Christ say, "Much has been forgiven her because she has loved much"?[20]

Not only Gregory, but also many of the Fathers taught this very thing before him. Ambrose says, "Tears do not demand forgiveness, but they do merit it."[21] St. Jerome, "Those who simply confess their sins merit mercy from the humility of the Savior."[22] Augustine says: "Remission of sins itself is not without any merit if faith obtains this. For the merit of faith is not nothing; by such faith he said: 'God be merciful to me, a sinner,' and he went down justified, faithful and humble."[23] And in another epistle: "If someone will have said that faith of a work merits grace we cannot deny, but freely confess that it is so."[24]

The last kind of works is of those that make a man justified and proceed from the indwelling of the Holy Spirit in the heart of man as well as charity diffused in it. To such works, whether you like it or not, we attribute merit. Not in the manner that the remission of sins (which precedes it) can properly fall under merit, but they truly and properly merit glory and eternal beatitude. Otherwise, why would Paul say: "I have fought the good fight, I have finished my course, I have kept the true faith, as to the rest there is laid up for me a crown of justice that the just Judge will render to me on that day"?[25] If eternal life is not truly the wages of good works, why does he call it the crown of justice, and not the gift of mercy? Why does he say it must

---

[19] Jonah 3:10.

[20] Luke 7:47.

[21] *In Lucam* lib. 10.

[22] Lib. 2 *adversus Pelagianos.*

[23] Epist. 105.

[24] Epist. 106.

[25] 2 Timothy 4:7

be rendered, not given? Why from the just judge, not from a generous king? Therefore, St. Augustine says: "Even eternal life itself, which at any rate will be enjoyed without end and consequently is given for merits that precede it, nevertheless, we are not sufficient in ourselves to furnish those very merits for which eternal life is given; rather we do these works by grace, it is even expressed by grace, but not because it is given by our merits, rather because the merits themselves are given, by which eternal life is given."[26]

Those two Scriptural testimonies that Chytraeus quoted hardly strike fear in us, namely: "I am the one who blots out iniquities... There is no salvation in any other." Testimonies of this sort exclude another God, another Christ, and another Savior and doctor of souls, which truly promise salvation without the true God and Christ Jesus the Savior. Nevertheless, they do not exclude faith, hope, charity, penance and the Sacraments, whereby the merit of Christ is applied to us, especially with God's operation. Otherwise, how could these two propositions adhere together: "I am the one who blots out iniquities; There is no salvation in any other," and "Your faith has saved you";[27] "He will save those who hope in him";[28] "He will save his soul";[29] "The fear of the Lord expels sin";[30] "He who will have believed and been baptized, will be saved";[31] "He who eats this bread will live forever?"[32] That is

---

26   Epistle 105.

27   Luke 7:50.

28   Psalm 36 (37).

29   Ezechiel 18:27

30   Sirach 1:21

31   Mark 16:16.

32   John 6:51, 58.

sufficient on this point; let us continue with Chytraeus.

III

The Gospel teaches that one who does penance and hears the promise ought to believe the promise and determine that the sins of others, such as Peter or Paul, and even his own are remitted on account of Christ. Such a man pleases God, is received and heard by God and by this faith he comes to God in daily invocation. The Popes contend that it always must be doubted whether we have remission of sins. Such a doubt is simply opposed to faith and is clearly heathen.

Our Gospel sufficiently teaches that it behooves one to have faith in the promises of God; all Catholics teach that there is no reason to doubt this. Still, there is no place in the Gospel where one can read that remission of sins is promised to men by God. Much less can one find that each and every man should determine for certain that his own sins are remitted or that he pleases God, is received by God or heard by him. Rightly so, because it would overturn the other passages in which one can very clearly read the contrary. For what could be more clear than what the wise man writes in Ecclesiastes: "There are the just and the wise, and their works are in the hand of God; still no man knows whether they are worthy of hatred or love."[33] Likewise it is clear from Job chapter IX: "Even if I were simple, is my soul ignorant of this?" And again: "I feared all my works, knowing that you would not spare the offender."?

What of the fact that nearly all divine promises have an

---

[33] Eccl. 9:1.

attached condition, which no man can know for certain whether he will have fulfilled them or not? "If you wish to enter into life, keep the commandments."[34] "If anyone comes to me and does not hate his father, and mother, and wife and children, brothers, sisters and still his own life, he cannot be my disciple."[35] "The Spirit himself gives testimony to our spirit, that we are sons of God; but if sons, then heirs, heirs of God, co-heirs of Christ, still, if we suffer it is so we will be glorified with him."[36] Next, St. Ambrose, who (as we said above) is much older than Gregory, says: "He wished the reproach that he suspected to be taken away from him, or else he thought in heart that God had not done so; although it was abolished by penance, still he suspected that his reproach still remained; and therefore he prayed to God that he would take it from him, because God alone knows what he cannot know even though he is the one who did it."[37]

IIII

The Gospel teaches that there is only one propitiatory sacrifice in the world (Hebrews 7:10), that Christ was offered once and for all to take away sins. The Popes teach that Christ is offered daily in the sacrifice of the Mass to God the Father."

Indeed the Gospel teaches that there is only one propitiatory sacrifice in the world because it was offered on the cross once and no Catholic denies that. Yet, the

---

[34] Matthew 19:17

[35] Luke 14:26.

[36] Romans 8:16.

[37] *in Psalmum* 118.

Gospel nowhere says that this unique sacrifice cannot daily be repeated in a mystery by Christ the High Priest through the hands of priests, and Catholics affirm this. Not only do they affirm it, those in all the centuries after Gregory, but so do all the Fathers that preceded him by many centuries. Let us take Augustine in the name of all the others, who said: "Was not Christ immolated once in himself? And still, in the Sacrament he is immolated for the people, not only through all the solemnities of Easter, but every day."[38]

V

The Gospel teaches that sin is not only external actions opposed to the law of God, but even doubts about God, carnal security and contumacy, as well as the concupiscence born with us, and cast off in rebirth (Romans 7). The Popes deny that these evils are cast off in rebirth [Baptism] and claim these are sins opposed to the law of God.

No Popes, that is, Catholics, teach that only external actions are sins; rather this is a lie that Chytraeus learned from his father, who does not stand in the truth. Moreover, we do not question whether doubts about God, carnal security, contumacy and concupiscence are sins if they are voluntary; but if they are involuntary, such as the lusts of the flesh against the spirit, which Paul sensed, even if he did not share in them, these we steadfastly deny are sins. We do not relate this concerning the Pauline words to the heretics as if the words of Paul are true for them and not or us, but concerning the interpretation of the words. Chytraeus should not take it too badly if we propose Augustine and the whole chorus of the saints against these

---

[38] Epist. 23 *ad Bonifacium.*

new men. Augustine says: "But concerning that concupiscence of the flesh of which they speak, I think that they are deceived, or that they deceive; for with this even he that is baptized must struggle with a pious mind, however carefully he presses forward, and is led by the Spirit of God. But although this is called sin, it is certainly so called not because it is sin, but because it is made by sin, as a writing is said to be some one's hand because the hand has written it.[39]

VI

The Gospel teaches that man can by no means satisfy the law of God in this imbecilic nature and that the just man in the perfect fulfillment of the law has committed every sin. (Romans 8). The sense of the enmity of the flesh is against God, for he does not obey the law of God, and cannot even do so. The Popes contend that man can satisfy the law of God and be just in this perfect fulfillment and merit eternal life.

The Popes, *i.e.* sons of the Catholic Church, do not say that man in this imbecility of nature has committed every sin. We acknowledge and profess it is very true what John says in the beginning of his epistle: "If we will have said that we have no sin, we deceive ourselves." Yet, these daily sins do not abolish justice, nor are against the law apart from the law of God, when for the remission of the same faults, "every spirit will pray in due season,"[40] and all the

---

[39] *Contra duas epistolas Pelagianorum*, lib. 1, cap. 13 (27).

[40] Psalm 31 (32):6. Translator's note: Here it must be noted that the Vulgate was revised subsequent to this work to read: "Pro hac orabit ad te omnis sanctus in tempore opportuno." Every one who is holy will pray for this in due season. The original that Bellarmine used is

just sons of God and saints daily are taught to say: "Forgive us our sins."[41] For that reason, we do not fear to assert that man can be justified by the grace of God, and fulfill the law by the assistance of the same grace and in that fulfillment merit eternal life. We know who said: "And his commandments are not heavy,"[42] and likewise "Call the workers and pay them the wage."[43] And again: "Come ye blessed of my Father and possess the kingdom prepared for you, etc., for they hungered and you gave them to eat."

For this reason Augustine says: "For it is certain that we keep the commandments if we will; but because the will is prepared by the Lord, we must ask of Him for such a force of will as suffices to make us act by the willing."[44] And again: "Therefore, grace is given not because we fulfill the law, but that we can fulfill the law."[45] Nor do the words of the Apostle trouble us: "The sense of the flesh is enmity opposed to God." The same Apostle had already said: "Therefore, I myself serve the law of God in mind, while the flesh serves the law of sin."[46] What we do in mind, we truly do, but what we do in the flesh, if it is opposed to the mind, it is not ours, just as the same Apostle says: "If I do what I refuse, I do not work it."

VII

The Gospel teaches that good works are merely those that were commanded by God, according to

---

maintained in the translation.

[41] Matth. 6:12.

[42] 1 John 5:3.

[43] Matth. 20:8.

[44] *De gratia et libero arbitrio*, cap. 16 (32).

[45] *De Spiritu et litera*, ca. 10.

[46] Romans 7:25.

the rule whereby he commands us only to those things ratified by the Lord, you shall not add nor take away. But the Popes ruin the whole Church with traditions, etc.

As if this had not been repeated by them and refuted a thousand times already. When he says this is contained in the Gospel that good works are only those which God commanded, it is false. Where, I ask, does God command virginity? Doesn't Paul say: "Moreover, concerning virgins I have no precept of the Lord."[47] and still he says in the same place that it is good to remain a virgin, "Therefore, he who marries a virgin does well, but he who does not does better."

And that rule does not help him much; the things that I command you, let only these be done for the Lord. Moreover, in that place God does not forbid something other than that we should break his precepts; rather we should keep them whole, just as he commanded them, not turning to the left or the right. Therefore, St. Augustine, distinguishing precepts from counsels, says: "For it cannot be said: You shall not marry, as it is said 'you shall not commit adultery,' or 'you shall not kill;' the latter are demanded, so they are offered. If the former is done, it is praised, but if the latter two should happen, they are condemned. In the latter the Lord commands us what is due, in the former if you will have overspent, he will render to you upon returning."[48]

VIII
The Gospel teaches that each part of the Sacrament

---

[47]   1 Cor. 7:25

[48]   *De sancta virginitate*, cap. 30.

of the Lord's supper must be administered to all Christians, and expressly from the chalice (Drink from this, all of you.) But the Popes decreed and defined otherwise.

Still we do not see that passage of the Gospel where we are taught that each part of the Sacrament must be administered to all Christians. For the Lord does not say: "Drink from this, all Christians", but "drink from this, all of you." And Mark explained who "all of you" might be when he added: "And they all drank from it." Moreover, not all Christians drank, but all the Apostles, who then alone supped with the Lord.

IX

The Gospel teaches that true penance, or conversion to God, is a grave sorrow of heart for sins, and faith establishing that his sins were certainly remitted by Christ, etc. On the other hand, even though the Popes number contrition among the parts of penance, nevertheless they feign that this remission of sins is merited, and add auricular confession that was not commanded by God, and satisfaction or works due in which they satisfy for the eternal punishments of sins, and this very thing they devise can be done for money. The whole doctrine is a blasphemy against the merit of the son of God, who alone satisfied for sins.

Here he proves nothing and advances no testimony of the Gospel. I see only inane words poured forth with an admixture of lies. For what he says on conversion and grave sorrow of heart he could omit. We truly require conversion and grave sorrow of heart among penitents, although he requires nothing else than I know not what terrors he has for contrition. What he adds on establishing faith for our sins to be remitted was refuted above. What he says about the Pope's contrition meriting remission of sins is a lie refuted above. When he says the Popes say that temporal satisfaction satisfies for eternal punishments it is equally a lie. For we do not think it satisfies for eternal punishments since we do not doubt it is remitted in justification, rather, God demands men who come to the Sacrament after Baptism to do penance for them either here or in purgatory. St. Augustine says: "The penalty is prolonged beyond the fault, lest, if the penalty were to end with the fault it would be accounted small."[49]

What he adds next about auricular confession not being commanded or that satisfaction is opposed to the merit of Christ is yet another case where he says it but does not prove it. Let him read, if he will, St. Cyprian[50] and he will discover the necessary confession of sin as well as satisfaction repeated in these very terms. Now, that money is paid out for satisfaction among Catholics (lest by chance here he might suspect some foul business) is nothing other than one kind of satisfaction, and it can be changed into a different kind by the judgment of the priest, such as fasting and almsgiving. Let us continue to the rest.

X

The Gospel teaches that one spouse is conceded to all men whether lay or priests, and it says eloquently that the prohibition of a spouse and of food is the doctrine of the devil. On the other hand the Popes forbid a spouse to a great part of men,

---

[49] Tract. *in Ioan.* 124, n.5.

[50] *de lapsis*, serm. 5.

priests and monks, and command them to abstain from certain foods on certain days.

Where, I ask, does the Gospel teach that a wife is conceded to those who have a vow of continence? Perhaps in Hebrews 13 where we read: "A spouse is honorable to all [men]." Moreover, if "in all" means absolutely every man, it will be honorable then for a father and daughter to marry, or mother and son, and brother and sister. Yet if Chytraeus does not like this, then he also should not like the idea that marriage would be honorable among a monk and a consecrated nun, or even with the rest of men to whom marriage is not lawful by vow. For the Apostle only means that we will honor marriage in all things when it is rightly and legitimately joined. Moreover it remains for Chytraeus to prove that those who make a vow of perpetual continence can duly and legitimately marry.

Listen to what Chrysostom wrote to a monk by the name of Theodore, who desired to marry or perhaps already had: "Honorable nuptials; but it is not now fitting for you to preserve the privilege of the married and although you frequently call this very thing nuptials, still, I reckon that it is worse than adultery."[51] Concerning that passage of the Apostle, 1 Timoth. 4: "Prohibiting to marry," etc., see what we said above in chapter 21 near the end.

XI

The Gospel teaches that there is one true and solid foundation upon which the Church of God is built, clearly our Lord Jesus Christ (1 Corinth. 3; Acts 4). That passage of Matthew 16 is so interpreted by St. Augustine (upon this rock), saying: 'You are Christ, the son of the living God; this is upon my very self,

---

[51] Epist. 6.

the son of the living God, I will build my Church; upon me I will build you, not me upon you. Yet the Popes cry out to the contrary that upon the rock of the Roman Church and the ordinary succession of Popes, the whole rest of the Church of the Christian world has been built.

But I believe he does not oppose Paul with himself, when he says: "We are built upon the foundation of Apostles and prophets."[52] Nor does he oppose Paul's assertion: "There is no foundation of the Church apart from Christ."[53] John, in the Apocalypse, ch. 21, when he says: "Twelve Apostles are the foundation of the twelve churches." For Paul speaks on the primary foundation in Corinthians, while he speaks in Ephesians (along with John in the Apocalypse) on the secondary foundations. Augustine speaks on the quality of the foundation in his *Narrations on the Psalms* against the position of the Donatists, where he says: "Count the priests, even from the See of Peter itself. That is the rock which the proud gates of hell do not conquer." But much more was said about this above in book I, ch. X.

XII

The Gospel teaches that no Apostle or bishop, or any minister of the Gospel, is superior to another, or has greater power and dominion in what pertains to ministry. Rather all ministers have equal power to teach the Gospel, administer Sacraments, bind criminals and absolve those doing penance, as Scripture teaches the keys of the kingdom were

---

[52] Ephes. 2:20.

[53] 1 Corinth. 3:11.

consigned to all the Apostles equally.[54] On the other hand, the Roman Pontiff boasts that he has supreme power over all other bishops and the whole Church, and carries both the spiritual and political sword by divine law, etc.

Where does the Gospel teach that one bishop or minister does not have greater power than another? I still have not found it. The places that he cites clearly show the contrary. In Luke 22 the Lord exhorts them to humility and forbids them the rule of kings, and also tyranny to those who ought to be in charge of the Church; still among the Apostles one was greater than the rest, nay more, the Lord affirms himself to be the leader of the others. For he says: "He who is greater among you, let him be made the lesser, and he who is excellent (in Greek this is ἡγούμενος, which means a general), let him be just as an attendant." Moreover, the Apostle, where he says that he planted and Apollo watered, and again he laid the foundation just like an architect, and others built,[55] doesn't he mean clearly enough that he is greater than Apollo and the rest of his helpers?

Hence, in John 20 it is said to all the Apostles "Behold, I send you and whoever's sins you will have forgiven, etc."; but in chapter 21 the Apostles and the rest of the faithful are subjected to St. Peter, as sheep to their pastor, since to Peter alone in the presence of the other Apostles did the Lord say: "Feed my sheep." Next, even if in Matthew 18 all the Apostles are indicated with the words "whatever you will have bound, etc.," still, when he said, "I will give you the keys of the kingdom, etc." he said it to Peter alone, and

---

[54] Luke 22:24-30, 1 Corinth. 3:4, John 20:21-23 and Matthew 18:18.

[55] 1 Cor. 3.

without a doubt the Lord did not promise something to him singly unless he also meant to show something singular to him. But on this we have said much above in Book I, chapters 12-14.

Now, to his objection against the two swords in Bonfiace VIII's teaching where he mocks the arguments of that Pontiff, it is best to respond with just one thing in this place. We will take everything from St. Bernard who was a holy man even in the estimation of Chytraeus, as well as the customary plea of Melanchthon and Calvin that we have heard more than once. See book 2 and 4 of *De Consideratione*, or if he would like, he could refer back to the very matter when we dealt with it in the last book on the Pope,[56] and this will suffice for Chytraeus' teaching on Antichrist.

Now we must briefly show that this very vision of John squares better with Luther and Lutherans. In the first place that star which fell from heaven to earth can signify Luther. It is clear since he went from a monk to a secular, from celibate to married, from poor he was made rich, and from sober and modest living to sumptuous dinners and lunches. What else is this than to have fallen from a heavenly way of life to an earthly one?

Next, the smoke from the well of the abyss that follows the fall is clearly the blind and stupid who have no sense. In that before Luther defected from the Catholic Church, nearly the whole West was of the same faith and religion and in whatever direction a man might go, he would always find his brethren. All were then in the light. But after the fall of Luther such a smoke of errors, sects and schisms rose out that now even in the same province, nay more, in the same city or even house, one does not recognize another.

---

[56] See Book V.

This smoke also obscured (as it says in the Apocalypse) the sun and air. By the sun we understand Christ, through the air the Scriptures, whereby we find, in a certain measure, our own as well as expose our adversaries. Indeed, Transylvania and its nearby regions are a witness of how vehemently this smoke has obscured, where they openly deny the divinity of Christ; Germany is also a witness, where Anabaptists openly and everywhere deny the humanity of Christ. Now truly there were once many heretics that attacked Christ in a similar fashion, but none more impudently than the heretics of this time. For not only do many of them deny that Christ is God, but they add he cannot be invoked nor can we do anything to know him. It is a horror to hear or read with what temerity the heretics of our age dispute the mysteries of Christ.

Again, it is incredible how vehemently this smoke has obscured the Scriptures. Now there are so many versions and commentaries extant that are opposed to one another that what was once clear now seems very obscure. What can be said more clearly than what Paul said, "I have no precept from the Lord on virgins, but I have counsel."[57] And yet all the heretics of our time constantly deny that there ever was a counsel of virginity and that Paul does not dare to counsel that one embrace virginity in this passage, but rather he simply wanted to discourage man. What can be said more plainly than the word of the Lord, "This is my body"? And yet nothing in this time is more obscure. What shall I say about the Transylvanians? They so pervert their commentaries on the Gospel of John (which was almost certainly written against Cherintus and Ebionus who denied the divinity of Christ) that they especially try to show from it that Christ is not God.

Now let us come to the locusts which come from the

---

[57] 1 Cor. 7:25.

smoke of the well. Chytraeus understands through locusts bishops, clergy and monks, but he gets it all wrong, for even before the times of Gregory there were bishops, clergy and monks in the Church; nevertheless these strange locusts had not yet arisen. All the things that John says about the locusts square very suitably with the Lutherans and the other heretics of our time. 1) Locusts always come in great numbers and usually fall in squadrons. "A locust does not have a king and all go out in squadrons."[58] So the Lutherans do not properly have one head since they deny that there is a head of the whole Church. Just the same, they rose in a very brief period to be a vast multitude and no wonder, for they open the door to all vice-filled men; the gluttons run to them, because the Lutherans establish no fasts; the incontinent likewise because they reject all vows of continence. They concede marriage to monks and priests—even consecrated nuns. Likewise all apostates flock to them because all the cloisters are reserved for them and converted into palaces. Greedy and ambitious princes, because they add Ecclesiastical goods to their person and even Ecclesiastical power, they become not only lazy but enemies of good works because among them faith alone suffices; good works are not necessary. Next, all the reprobate and criminals flock to them because they have lifted them from the necessity to confess their sins and give an account to their own pastor, which is usually a bridle to sinners. Hence the locusts have so multiplied.

Moreover, these locusts are described by St. John in a paradoxical fashion. For they are said to have a human face, and even that of a women, the tail of a scorpion, the body of a locust, likewise they wear a crown on their head seeming to be of gold, but they have the teeth of lions and

---

[58] Proverbs 30:27.

their chest is armed with an iron cuirass. Next, they seem just as horses prepared to battle and once they hear that the alarm has been sounded as the sound of chariots running to war, they had over themselves the king, the angel of the abyss, who is called the exterminator.

The charming faces mean the beginning of their preaching since it always begins from the Gospel. They promise to say nothing but the purest Word of God. This is how they so easily attract the more simple. The tail of the scorpion means a poisonous and deadly outlet, for after they proposed the Word of God they foul it up with perverse interpretation, just as a recoiled tail drives in the sting and the lethal venom is found. The body of the locust is almost nothing other than the stomach (for it is a large-bellied insect) and therefore it can neither advance nor fly correctly, but raises itself high by jumping and soon falls to earth. This means the heretics of this time are men addicted to their stomach, enemies of fasting and continence, and therefore can neither advance to the way of the commandments nor fly to contemplate heavenly things.

Certainly they try to raise themselves at some point and amend their morals, but after the fashion of locusts, soon they fall back to earth. The Saxon visitation can serve as an example. Luther noticed that on account of the "gospel liberty" that they had preached all laws of the Church were abrogated and the people, deprived of that bridle, rushed into sin. Therefore, he established the visitation and advised pastors to preach penance, fear of God, obedience and good works. Still, this accomplished nothing.[59]

For equal reason they try to fly through contemplation and already have written everywhere books on the Trinity,

---

[59] See Cochlaeus in the life and acts of Luther, MDXXVII.

on the Incarnation, and on other mysteries of this sort; but they fall into very serious errors, nay more, pernicious heresies, which is clear from the Ubiquists, who destroy the whole mystery of the Incarnation and the Trinity.[60]

The crowns on the head of the locusts mean the arrogance and pride by which they raise themselves over all men. There is a book of Luther extant which was written to Duke George, in which he says, "No doctor or writer from the time of the Apostles, nor even any theologian or canon lawyer has confirmed, instructed and consoled the consciences of those in the lay state as remarkably and beautifully *as I have*. Through a singular grace of God I know this for certain, because neither Ambrose nor Augustine, who are the best in this matter, are equal to me in this." What? Not only do Luther and Calvin make nothing of a thousand Cyprians and a thousand Augustines, but each Lutheran clergyman also holds Papists for asses and whipping posts! Were these the crowns that are just as gold—that is they seemed like gold but were not? They feign themselves full of zeal for the honor of God and moved by charity to say the things they say, when still they are less than acquainted with the zeal of God.

The teeth of the lion mean the detractions with which they assiduously slander the repute of Pope, clergy and monks by letters and sermons, as well as the saints themselves who rule in beatitude with God. And they seem to be nurtured by detractions since they make so many which are not, nor have been and perhaps never, that they appear to be utterly devoid of conscience. It is clear enough

---

[60]   Translator's note: The Ubiquists (*ubiquisti*) were a branch of Lutherans founded by Brenz that theld the Eucharist, the body of Christ was everywhere because Christ's flesh had been deified. This doctrine persisted until the Thirty Years War.

both from the other things which are read everywhere in their books and from those which a little before we cited in the Smalchaldich council, in Illyricus, Tilman, Calvin and Chytraeus.

The chest armed with an iron breastplate means obstinacy. Our adversaries are so obdurate that even if they were clearly beaten in argument, they will still never yield. Often they prefer to die than to recede from their obstinacy.

The similitude of the horses who seem prepared for war means boldness and temerity. They boldly challenge all to war, even though afterward they only advance a great many lies for argument. Luther said: "Come here all you papists, put together all of your studies and untie this knot if you can."[61] Nearly all the others speak in the same way. But the similitude of the swift chariots means the speed whereby that new heresy uses those possessed of different regions. In short order they occupied not only many kingdoms in the North, but even dared to sally to India, although God did not permit them establish themselves there, since the new and tender parts of the Church of Christ have not yet merited such a scourge.

Next, the angel of the abyss is called the king of these locusts, because even if locusts do not have a visible king, as we noted above, nevertheless, they have an invisible one since they cannot lack the devil as, "He is the king of all the sons of pride."[62] Moreover, the king of the locusts is called the exterminator because the devil never exterminated and devastated the Church through heresy as much as through Lutherans. For a great many of the other heresies destroyed one or another point of faith, but

---

[61] *Assertio* art. 25.

[62] Job 41:34.

did not overturn all order and discipline in the Church. But the Lutheran heresy partly by itself, and partly by its daughters, Anabaptism, Calvinism, Trinitarianism and Libertinism, have altogether destroyed all goods of the Church in those areas where they prowl. They removed the Trinity from God through the new Samosatens, who also removed divinity from Christ; through the Anabaptists the whole cult and invocation from the angels and saints, the suffrage of the living in purgatory; nay more, they clearly dismissed purgatory itself. From the Church on earth, they removed books of the divine Scripture, nearly all the Sacraments, all traditions, priesthood, sacrifice, vows, fasting, feast days, churches, altars, reliquaries, crosses, images, all monuments of piety and likewise Ecclesiastical laws, discipline, and they have also overturned all order.

Only hell remains, but perhaps it spared that lest it would do any injury to its king, the angel of the abyss. Not even this is the case, for many Lutherans deny that hell is a true place and fabricate I know not what sort of imaginary hell, but we spoke of this in Christ's descent into hell in another place.[63] Therefore, truly this can be called the exterminating heresy and a worthy title, which in Hebrew is אבדו [Abadon], in Greek is ἀπολλύων, and in Latin *exterminans*. It should be no wonder if not even the Lutherans themselves marvel at this utter destruction except that, as we have said, they have been blinded by the smoke.

Still, there is one consolation amidst so many evils, that (as John says) these locusts do not harm the grass and the green trees; but only men who do not have the sign of the living God. Although that heresy may be wholly carnal, it

---

[63] See Bellarmine, *De Christo*.

cannot easily deceive good men in the souls of whom religion and piety have taken root and flourished. So we see rarely, or it has never happened, that some Church defected from the Lutherans that had not already begun to be corrupted among the lives of Catholics. But that is enough on this business.

CHAPTER XXIV

The Arguments of Calvin and Illyricus are Refuted, Where the Former Tries to Show the Pope is no Longer a Bishop, and the Latter on the Fable of "Pope Joan"

I T only remains that we prove what we had proposed as the last place, that the Roman Pontiff is not only not Antichrist, but that he has not lost his pontificate in any way. Calvin attempts to show by means of a certain conjecture that today he is not a true bishop, saying: "I should like to know what quality of a bishop the Pope himself might have? 1) The office of a bishop is to instruct the people in the Word of God; 2) The next is to administer the Sacraments 3) admonish and exhort, to correct those who are in fault and restrain the people by whole discipline. Now, which of these things does he do? Nay more, which of these things does he pretend to do? Let them say then, on what ground they will have him to be regarded as a bishop when he does not even resemble any part of the duty with his smallest finger.

"It is not with a bishop as with a king. The latter, if he were not to execute the proper duty of a king, nevertheless, he retains the title and the honor. Yet, in judgment about a bishop, the command of Christ is regarded, which ought to always avail in the Church. Let the Papists then untie this knot. I deny that their pontiff is the prince of bishops, seeing that he is no bishop."

Unless I am mistaken, the whole argument can be reduced to a syllogism. Since there is this difference between a bishop and a king, that the king is the name of a power and a prefecture to which is connected the duty of ruling the people, whereas the bishop is the name only of an office to minister the Word of God and the Sacraments; certainly then, if neither king nor bishop exercise their office then the name of king retains its dignity while the name of bishop loses it. Moreover, the Roman Pontiff does not even exercise the episcopal office in any clear manner, seeing that he does not preach the Word of God to the people or administer the Sacraments; therefore the Roman Pontiff has lost the name and dignity and thus cannot be called a bishop.

Moreover, the Centuriators attempt to confirm this conjecture of Calvin's with a sign. They say that the evident sign of the change of the Roman Church into the whore of Babylon was something God willed near those times in which this change took place, that a certain woman who was a harlot would sit in the Papal seat, who was called Pope John VIII.

They attempt to show this, 1) from the authors Platina, Martin Polonus, Sigebert and Marianus Scotus; 2) from the vestiges of the affair which still remain in our time. Without a doubt there is a certain seat made of porphyry that is perforated on the inside, which remains in the palace of St. John Lateran that they say was established for use after the scandal was detected so that it would be discovered whether one recently created Pope was a man or not. Likewise, from a certain statue of a woman with a boy that remained even to our own times in that place, where it says the woman John VIII gave birth. Next, from the fact that the Roman Pontiffs, when they go from the Vatican to the Lateran, usually turn their head away at the place where this woman is said to have given birth in detestation of the fact; otherwise that is a straight road. It is not difficult, however, to untie these knots.

First we shall respond to Calvin. He is either talking

about the signification of the name, or about the thing itself, when he says that *bishop* is the name of an office, but *king* is the name of a dignity. If the former, then he is clearly deceived, since a bishop is called from the Greek ἐπισκοπειν (to consider or inspect) and it means the duty of overseeing. In the same way a king (*rex*) is called from ruling (*regendo*) and means the office of ruling. Just as king is the name of a magistrate, so also is ἐπίσκοπος among the pagans, for whom the name meant a magistrate, that is a *praetor*.[1] What is more, the Holy Scripture attributes to a bishop the name of shepherd and king.[2]

But if Calvin speaks on the matter itself, then he is no less deceived. Just as royal authority is not a simple office to judge, as a judge of others, but is a true prefecture in political matters (the power to rule men subjected to him by commands and punishments); so also the episcopate is not a simple office to preach, as it is for others who preach yet are not pastors, but is a true ecclesiastical prefecture that has the power to rule men in spiritual and divine matters—hence to command and punish. We have spoken about that matter and many others above, and we will have much to say elsewhere. For the moment, a few passages will suffice to make the matter crystal clear. The Apostle Paul teaches: "As for the rest, when I come I will distribute it."[3] "Therefore, I write these things being absent because being present I will deal much more severely, according to the power that the Lord has given me."[4] And in Hebrews he says: "Obey those who have been placed

---

[1] Aristophanes, *Birds.*

[2] Isaiah 44; Ephes. 4.

[3] 1 Cor. 11:34.

[4] 2 Cor. 13:10.

over you and be subject to them."[5] Again, in 1 Timothy he says: "Do not receive an accusation against a priest unless it is with two or three witnesses."[6] Besides, it is also false that Popes do not exercise episcopal office. For they are not held to give sermons and minister the Sacraments *per se*, if they are impeded by some just cause; rather it is sufficient if they will see to it that these things are done by others. Otherwise bishops would be obliged to do the impossible, since there is no place so scanty that a bishop can suffice by himself to preach and minister the Sacraments through the whole diocese. Therefore, just as it satisfies if he will preach through another in some place where he cannot be present, so also it satisfies if he will preach in every place through others when there is no way he could be present there. We do not lack the examples of antiquity. Possidius writes that St. Valerius, the bishop of Hippo, commissioned St. Augustine in the duty of preaching when he was still a priest, because being a Greek he could not preach to the people in Latin.[7] Possidius also relates that in the Eastern Church a great many bishops customarily demanded from their priests that they take up the office of preaching which they could not carry out by themselves. Nevertheless we cannot say that either S. Valerian or others who did not preach the Word of God themselves were not bishops.

Now what the Centuriators say, 1) That Sigebert, Marianus Scotus are more ancient than Martin Polonus, and, they place a "Pope Joan"[8] in their *Chronicles* is

---

[5]   Hebrews 13:17.

[6]   1 Tim.. 5:19.

[7]   *Vita S. Augustini.*

[8]   Translator's note: The Latin reads "*Papa Ioannes foemina*", but for the sake of ease we have rendered it with the more familiar "Joan" in English. In Latin Ioannes is a 3rd declension noun and will have the

altogether false. Even if this is discovered in the printed versions of Sigebert and Marianus Scotus, it is not discovered in the most ancient manuscripts, it is certain that these authors' testimonies are corrupted. The most ancient example of Sigebert's manuscript is still extant from the monastery of Gembloux where he was a monk. It is reckoned to be in Sigebert's own hand and he makes no mention of a "Pope Joan." John Molanus, a Doctor of Louvain that is still alive, is a witness to the example of this manuscript. Likewise, in the most ancient copies of Marianus Scotus a "Pope Joan" cannot be found. The edition of the *Metropoli* of Albert Kranz published in 1524 at Cologne witnesses the fact.

2) Next, it is proved from his own narration that Martin Polonus fabricated this particular tale about "Pope Joan." a) He says this Joan was English from Moguntia. But Moguntia is not in England but in Germany. The Centuriators tell it the other way around, that she was Moguntian but raised in England. Moreover, Theodore Bibliander says in his *Chronicle* that she was not from England at all but merely educated there.

b) Martin and those who follow him says that she devoted herself to letters in Athens. But it is certain in that time there was no academy of letters in Athens or anywhere else in Greece. Synesius writes in his last epistle to his brother that in his time Athens was nothing, but he lived just after the times of St. Basil and St. Gregory Nazianzen. Cedrenus and Zonaras write in the lives of the emperors Michael and Theodora, around the end of the reign of Michael when he ruled by himself after he banished his mother Theodora, that schools of philosophy and good letters were restored by Bardas Cesar, when even to that time all studies of wisdom had been extinguished in

---

same endings for masculine and feminine.

Greece for a great many years, so much so that not even a vestige remained. It is certain that the reign of Michael by himself fell in the times of Pope Nicholas I who succeeded Benedict III, who succeeded this pretended Joan, that is the woman John VIII which they allege. Furthermore, all histories, even that of Bibliander, place the beginning of the reign of Michael alone in the year 856, while the pontificate of this Joan would have been 854. It follows then that after the death of this Joan education was beginning to revive in Greece.

c) The Centuriators say that this Pope Joan gave birth on a journey from the Vatican to inspect the Church of the Lateran. But it is a certain fact, as Onuphrius proves in a book on the seven churches, that the Roman Pontiffs did not live in the Vatican, but in the Lateran palace even to the times of Boniface IX, that is even to 1390. How, therefore, if she lived in the Lateran, would she want to go from the Vatican to inspect the Lateran? Certainly if anyone were to write today that the Pope went from the Lateran to inspect the Church of the Vatican, it would be ridiculous, since everyone knows the Pope lives in the Vatican.

d) Martin and the others who follow him say this Joan gave birth during a solemn and public service. But this has no probability because a woman that was so many months with child would in no wise wish to proceed since there was a greatest danger of being detected.

3) This same thing is proven from an epistle of Leo IX, a very serious Pope, to Michael the bishop of Constantinople, where Pope Leo writes that the constant report is in the patriarchate of Constantinople that many eunuchs sat and among these a woman had crept in and was patriarch.[9] Leo IX certainly would never have

---

[9] Cap. 23.

mentioned this to the Greeks if such a thing had happened in the Roman See. Nay more, this is perhaps the root of the fable about Pope Joan. Since there was a rumor that some woman was the bishop of Constantinople, and then little by little, the name of Constantinople was dropped but the opinion and report of a female pontiff remained, and a universal Pontiff at that, some began to say in hatred of the Roman Church that the woman was the Roman Pontiff. And it has the appearance of truth that this rumor arose in the times of Martin. Certainly Martin Polonus, who first wrote this, relates no author but only says it is related. Therefore he has this only from an uncertain rumor.

Nor should it be any wonder if someone would fabricate this fable in hatred of the Roman Church, after the foundation about a female Pontiff had been laid amid the greatest contentions that existed in that time between emperors and Popes. For even now we see that the Centuriators fabricate more incredible things. Martin only wrote that this women was English from Moguntia, and added nothing about her parents, or even the woman's proper name. Nevertheless, the Centuriators have felt free to add in the rest of the details, saying that her father was an English priest and that at first she was called Gilberta, and raised in the habit of a man in the monastery of Fuldensis, and that she wrote many books on sorcery. These are all merely fabrications without any witness and devised without reason. Add that Martin Polonus appears to have been very simple, since he wrote many other fables as if they were attested history.

Now what they say about the perforated seat, the statute of the woman and the turning aside on the road are easily answered. It is certain from the book of sacred ceremonies that there were three stone seats in the Lateran Basilica in which a new Pope sat in the time of his coronation.[10] The first seat was before the entrance to the Church and this was low and abject; to such a seat a new Pope was lead and sat somewhat, to show by that ceremony that he ascends from the lowest place to the highest. From there elevating him they sung what we read in 1 Kings 2: "*Suscitat de pulvere egenum, et de stercore erigit pauperem, ut sedeat cum principibus et solium gloriae teneat.*"[11] And this is the reason why these were called the seats of the dung hill. The second seat was made of porphyry in the palace itself, and there he sat a second time in the sign of possession, and also sitting there he received the keys of the Church in the Lateran Palace. The third seat was similar to the second and not far from it, and also sitting it in after a short time, he handed the same keys to the one from whom he had received them, perhaps that this ceremony would remind him of death through which in a short time he was going to hand that power to another. From that seat, to the discovery of his actual sex, there is never a mention.

But the statue of the woman with the child without a doubt was not Pope Joan. For if our adversaries say that ancient historians refused to place the memory of this event in their books, how does it have the appearance of truth that the Popes themselves would have wanted to remember it with a statue? Next, if the statue was of "Joan," it would represent a woman with a little infant just born, but the image relates neither a woman, nor an infant she was bearing in her bosom, but a boy sufficiently large and several years old as if going before a servant. For that reason some men think it was a statue of some heathen

---

[10] *Sacrarum Ceremoniarum,* lib. 1, sec. 2.

[11] "He raises the poor man out of the dust, the beggar out of the dung pile to sit among the princes and take hold of the throne of glory." 1 Kings (Samuel) 2:8.

priest prepared to sacrifice which his minister went before. Next, why the Popes omit the shorter way when setting out for the Lateran is not in detestation of any scandal but because that way is narrow and bent and it is usually very busy. Add that, as Onuphrius witnesses, there are plenty of Popes that have never once traveled on this road.

Finis